Getting TO KNOW You

A BOOK ON MARITAL STEPS WITH INFORMATION ABOUT MARRIAGE

ELVIS IRUH

authorHOUSE

AuthorHouse™ UK
1663 Liberty Drive
Bloomington, IN 47403 USA
www.authorhouse.co.uk
Phone: UK TFN: 0800 0148641 (Toll Free inside the UK)
*   UK Local: 02036 956322 (+44 20 3695 6322 from outside the UK)*

Published by AuthorHouse 10/09/2020

ISBN: 978-1-6655-8084-7 (sc)
ISBN: 978-1-6655-8085-4 (e)

To all men and women who believe in the sanctity of the
institution of marriage as holy to God.

To all my siblings, my supportive family, my spiritual children, and my good friends who
believe in my God-given talents. You bring out the best in me. Without you, I am nobody.

CONTENTS

FOREWORD

It was late in the afternoon when I received a call in my office from Pastor Elvis Iruh. "Would you like to write a foreword for my book *Getting to Know You*?"

"Sure. It would be my privilege," I answered. I wanted to know more about the book.

"I will mail it to you for reading," Pastor Elvis said.

I must admit that I was highly encouraged by his skilful writing as I went through the material.

I was recently reminded by Pastor Elvis during his and his wife's visit to my house that I was the first person he had informed and had asked for advice when he began dating his now wife, Sandra. Today they stand strong and firm as proven husband and wife with strong values and principles rooted in the Word of God. We live in a time where biblical values, both in marriage and in Christian dating, are becoming a matter of feelings rather than being based on what God says about these things. The divorce rate is at an all-time high among Christians, as it is among non-Christians. Many get into marriage on the basis of feelings, and when the feelings are gone, those people are also gone from the marriage. I believe people in relationships must be well informed and prepared for their marital journey in order to reduce casualties and preserve the home foundation for the future. Whilst most focus on the excitement of their wedding, which is great, they must also be equipped to remain excited for the rest of their journey. This can only happen by giving them the right tools for embarking on their marriage. I am therefore very pleased to see Pastor Elvis's contribution to that.

I do agree with his statement that *Getting to Know You* is not a claim to full authority on marriage counselling, but a contribution in helping would-be couples to have a better understanding of their premarriage engagement. However, I highly recommend this book to all for the purpose of godly living and healthy relationships. In the Netherlands, where I live and work as a pastor, we are known as a nation of tolerance. We face the challenge of premarriage living together among believers just like in many other parts of the world, and I believe that we can teach soundly on it without condemning anyone. This is our responsibility as ministers. Whilst we cannot force anyone to change, we must help people come to the biblical understanding of healthy Christian relationships. Lots of consistency and patience will be needed if results are to be achieved.

I still have a vivid mental image of the day when Pastor Elvis, his wife, Sandra, and their two daughters were officially sent out to Kenya to start a Victory Outreach church. Under the leadership of their still senior pastor, Roel van Rooij, for them it was a moment of excitement, truth, and challenge. For Pastor Elvis, he left the journalism profession and the magazine *The*

Voice—his business—behind in order to fully engage with God's Word and God's people of other cultures. I knew it wasn't going to be easy, but I also knew God would see them through. Sure enough the moments of loneliness came in, along with a sense of abandonment and discouragement, misunderstandings, a great deal of need with fewer resources to work with, and many other things. But I am very blessed to see how they stood firm, overcame the obstacles, built the church, and developed leaders for God's kingdom. That's why *Getting to Know You* is written not only from knowledge but also from experience and, therefore, is worth reading. It's easily readable and quite inspiring for someone seeking godliness. Pastor Elvis's teaching ability and his perspectives on biblical principles are highly motivating. Buy the truth and sell it not, is a wise phrase from the book of Proverbs.

As a pastor and confidant, I, together with my wife, am gladly honoured to be a part of the lives and ministry of Pastor Elvis and Sandra. I believe this book will minister health to the body of believers who feed on it. That is why I recommend to everyone who aspires to have a great marital and premarital relationship to read it.

Felix Asare, Regional Pastor
Victory Outreach Den Haag
The Netherlands
2020

PREFACE

Getting to Know You is a marriage guidebook for couples who intend to marry or couples who are already married.

My book is not in any way a claim to full authority on marriage counselling; however, it does seek to help would-be couples to have a better understanding of the things their relationship must have before they marry. *Getting to Know You* incorporates my personal experience with people and a research project I carried out during my six years' stay in Kenya. I discovered that modern courtship among Christian men and women is on the decline; fewer than 25 per cent of the African men I interviewed were interested in my subject of "getting to know you". Their partners (girlfriends) were of the opinion that they would naturally get to know each other better when they were married. It is to me a wrong assumption that needs to be corrected through this book. In fact, some are blinded simply on the basis that they are both "Christians", as they claim, and therefore their marriage will just work out fine. Yet it is a well-known fact that divorce among Christians is on the increase now more than ever before. This is not a good enough reason to go into marriage; many who have blindly followed this path have seen their marriages beset with problems within a matter of days—months at the most. The simple reason for the problem is that the two did not know enough about each other before rushing into marriage. Knowing that marriage is a lifelong commitment, I think it is necessary to contribute in any way to reduce the number of divorce cases among Christians.

Getting to Know You serves as a practical guide, providing simple discussions to help you through the journey leading up to marriage. And if you are already married, you probably will identify what you missed and begin to work on those things. It is never too late to work on your marriage. This book will help your family members, friends, colleagues, and even children who are growing into adulthood not to make the same mistakes as their parents.

You must realize that marriage is not a gamble or a contract on a piece of paper. Rather, it is a relationship built on the understanding and trust of two persons who profess to love each other.

Getting to Know You is for both the man and the woman. In fact, it is a book with many practical exercises you can share and do together as man and woman. Also include is guidance to help pastors and church marriage counsellors on how to advise people who plan to marry.

Having said this, I have the good example of my spiritual father and mother, Pastor Roel and Ida van Rooij, who have been married for over thirty-six years; they have known each other for more than fifty-six years. I have learnt much from them in my years in ministry, serving under them; they have guided their three children to successful marriages. With that experience, I went to Kenya to pastor a Victory Outreach International church in 2006. During those years, I was blessed with a lot of young men and young women in the church, but that of course came with its challenges. Most of them were not married or living together. A few others were in dating relationships, and one or two had lived together in a relationship, resulting in their having had children together. It seems a difficult subject to talk about or address in the church. However, this challenge prompted me to start writing about my experiences and the wisdom God gave me to help these couples. It was not enough just to inform them to get married; I also thought it vital to help them to stay married. I felt the need to help these young men and women come to know each other better so that they would not ultimately base their marriage on custom and tradition, but instead on the true love they had for each other as man and woman under godly principles and rules.

Another category of people I encountered were adults who had lived together for years (ten years or more) and yet were not married, neither by law nor before God. Simply put, this type of situation is the result of ignorance. These people assumed that because they had lived together for that long, their relationship was automatically a marriage; even some countries permit such a relationship and recognize it as marriage. I knew I had to do something about this problem before it became a thread in the church. With this in mind, I organized my first marriage seminar with my pastor friends Dr George Kennedy and his wife, Elizabeth Kennedy.

I knew it was only a matter of time before we would have wedding bells ringing in the church. Many came to speak to me after the seminar to ask questions on how they could regularize their relationships. I went on to tie five marital knots in our church and to preside over three other weddings outside our church. And I participated in other weddings organized by other pastors in and outside my city, Kisumu, which is in Kenya. I became known as the Marriage Pastor. I was invited as a guest to many wedding ceremonies in Kenya. I preferred to attend wedding ceremonies over other ceremonies. This is one of the reasons I was motivated to write *Getting to Know You*. So, within a period of five years, I had participated in at least twelve marriages. With some of these, I directly discipled the persons myself; their stories make up a part of this book. Others were done by Pastor Steve and his wife.

Why did many of these people agree to be married? Simply put, because they now had more information, more open communication, a more open mind, and a better attitude towards learning things they hadn't ever known before. After detailed counselling and motivation, these people agreed to get married rather than live together. Some of the stories are worth sharing so that others may learn from them.

Each of these people has an extraordinary story to tell, ranging from previous experience to near-quit situations. They made it past these obstacles, and they are happier for it today.

Know that marriage is an institution from which no one ever graduates. The more ideas we have about it, and the more knowledge we share about it, the better it is for a world that is gradually losing its values concerning marriage.

ACKNOWLEDGEMENTS

Several people contributed to help make this work become a reality. I sincerely wish to thank my wife, Sandra Iruh-Monsels, for her unwavering love and support from the very beginning. To my loving and immaculate queens, Deborah and Esther, a great many thanks to you both for allowing Papa to work late nights, thereby taking away some of the precious time I otherwise would have had to spend with you ladies. To Risper Isioma Membo and Anthony Ouma Iruh (my adopted children).

My sincere appreciation to my dear friends Elizabeth Kameo, Rev. Edgar Victor, David Banjoko, Bishop Dawn Willis, Pastor Sarah Mwangi, Uche Ideho, Xavier t' Zand, and Ifeyinwa Ezeagabu, among many others.

My sincere thanks to all members of Victory Outreach Church Kenya who gave me the chance to be a part of their lives and to the multitude of wonderful people I met during my six years' stay in Kenya and during my visits to Uganda. I need not list your names as you all know yourselves. Many thanks for the positive advice, criticisms, and even attacks, for it all aided in shaping me for the better.

I wish to thank all my spiritual children whom God has allowed me to mentor, guide, and coach in Kenya to the point of their weddings. Today they have established marriages. Their marriages are enduring and are blessed. I have been in touch with some of them, while others regularly inform me of their progress and share with me the joy of the decision they made some years back.

I wish to thank the following persons: Cliffe Ombogo Oduor and Terry Millicent Abong'o, now Mr and Mrs Cliff Oduor; Pastor Kevin Omondi Owino and Elizabeth Odera, now Pastor and Pastor Omondi; Dr Kevin Omamo Ndai and Carolyne Adienge, now Dr and Mrs Kevin Omamo Ndai; Tony Omondi Alaka and Emma Magwaro, now Mr and Mrs Anthony Alaka; Isaac and Sylvia Abuya (Dominion Chapel, Kisumu), now Mr and Mrs Isaac Abuya; Samuel Elisha and Eppy Achieng John (King's Assembly Church, Kisumu), now Mr and Mrs Samuel Elisha; Captain Thomas and Idah Agba of Mountain of Fire Ministries, Nairobi, now Captain and Mrs Thomas Agba; Francis and Nancy Kiogi, now Mr and Mrs Francis Kiogi, from Navasha, Kenya; Pastor George and Juliet Ochieng in Eldoret; and Mr Titi Godfrey and Loretta Achieng, now Mr and Mrs Titi Godfrey. I left Kenya to return to Europe a week before the wedding of Titi and Loretta, but they have allowed me to give them marriage counselling. Some of the material in *Getting to Know You* was used with them.

I salute you all, and I say thank you.

And special thanks to my spiritual parents, Pastor Roel and Ida van Rooij, whose insight and vision gave me the push to go to Kisumu, Kenya, on a mission. I probably would not have gone on my own without their encouragement as spiritual parents; they stood with me in all truth and faith during my stay in Kenya.

I thank my parents, Pa Sam Iruh (Uncle Sam) and Mama Suzie Omoroje (Mama Titi), for their love and understanding, and for handling this tough boy and nourishing me into who I am now. Now I know who I am.

And above all, my special thanks to my Lord and Saviour, Jesus Christ, the author and finisher of my faith, my beginning and my end, and the source of all good things that I have experienced in life.

Thank you all.

Almere, 2020

*   *   *

I have the consent of all persons featured herein to use their stories to encourage readers of *Getting to Know You*:

- Teaching materials from Victory Outreach International
- Victory Education and Training Institute (VETI)
- Registrar of Societies, African Christian Marriage and Divorce Act (1968)

CHAPTER 1

Introduction

In early March 2006, I was on a flight from Amsterdam, on my way to Kisumu, Kenya, with my wife, Sandra, and our two lovely daughters, Deborah and Esther Iruh, on a missionary journey with no specific date of return to our base in Europe. Of course with excitement, enthusiasm, and a little bit of caution, we set off for Kisumu, Kenya. On our arrival, we were impressed with what we saw and quickly settled down to work. We witnessed the tremendous moving of God in the church, but we also witnessed a lot of things that could be improved. One of these areas was relationships. We hardly could recognize married couples in the church; the men sat separately from the women, and husband and wife never walked together. It was a culture that needed to be addressed and changed as soon as possible.

My senior pastor, Roel van Rooij, had warned me to investigate the relationships in the church to discover if they were true marriages or if the couple were living together, as such was common in Kenya. Later that year, while talking to members of the congregation, I discovered that many people who claimed to be married couples were not. In fact, they were mostly living together and had started families, so they could no longer see the significance of marriage. Even men and women with titles and positions in the church were not customarily or officially married, and certainly not before the eyes of God. I thought it was time to deal with this issue.

God gave me the grace to share with these people the possibility of being wed once they had done what they needed to do first: get to know each other better. From that point on, the title of this book remained on my mind. I believe deep down inside that two people who profess to love each other need to come to know each other better before advancing the relationship to marriage. The chance of their marriage's surviving the storms of life is brighter and higher than it is for those who ignorantly go into marriage simply because they think it is something they have to do to be happy or to make the other person happy. Or it is customarily thought that when you come of age and you have the means, you should get married then. I think that marriage is a special union, so it is something you have to pray over, think over, and meditate on in order to come to the resolution that it is something you want for your life. At that point, you are ready to make the necessary commitment to remain married throughout the course of your lifetime. You may choose not to marry; if so, you will not be offending God as long as you live a holy life thereafter.

I recorded eight marriages within a period of five years in our church and a few others in other churches in Kenya. I organized marriage seminars for singles and couples, and they were well attended. My encounter with Pastor Eric Swenson of PEFA Christ Church Kisumu, sharing and comparing notes, made my desire to write *Getting to Know You* even greater. It has taken such a long time to get the book ready, but it is long and good. Wait to get married, because what I have to say within these pages will benefit your marriage. If you are already married or if you are currently planning to wed, *Getting to Know You* will serve as a good companion guide just to check how well you are prepared for this journey of life and how well you are doing on the journey so far.

Finally, late in 2018, after helping a friend to edit his book, I thought it was time to complete my book and use it to be a blessing to the younger generation so desperate for direction. Despite some of the delays (divine, I believe), *Getting to Know You* is the outcome, ready for you to read and be blessed by.

I did start and stop several times along the way as I was writing. But finally the book is ready and here for you. Read it for yourself, and also kindly share it with others, for marriage is a good thing to desire.

CHAPTER 2

Genesis of Getting to Know You

Pastor Eric and Gloria Swenson were coworkers in the vineyard of God in Kisumu, Kenya, with my wife and me. They were pastors of Christ Church in Kisumu, where they had lived and ministered for over thirty years. They returned to Australia just as I was preparing to return to the Netherlands after completing my missionary assignment in that same city in 2011.

The four of us—Pastor Eric and his wife, and I and my wife—shared a common burden on the subject of marriage. We noticed that many young adults were no longer contemplating marriage; rather, they had chosen the option of living together. In fact, upon my assumption as pastor of Victory Outreach Kenya, my sending pastor, Roel Van Rooij, asked me to investigate any members of my church congregation who claimed to be married. Many of them were not married but were living together, and naturally they had children together. They had just come to the conclusion that since they lived together, they were married. Of course this is not true. Pastor Eric and his wife made a manual to guide would-be couples in the steps they would have to take if they intended to become husband and wife in his church. We had a situation where a brother from my church was interested in a sister in his church, and for that reason, Pastor Eric and I came together to prepare notes on how to guide these two people successfully into making the final decision to become husband and wife. It was the first time he could remember that a co-pastor had agreed to counsel two separate persons from two different churches on the same subject: marriage. My wife and I shared ideas with Pastor Eric and his wife. We made notes, and along with what he had written, I decided to create a guide to share with would-be couples to encourage them and educate them on steps they would need to take if they planned to get married someday. I shared my notes with the Swensons, and they gave me their approval to use their materials to support young men and women who desire to get married. After having used the manual for five years in Kenya, I became convinced that it would be better put in book form so that people may have a copy for themselves. After a long period of marriage, you can share it others or revisit it once in a while to keep your marriage alive, refreshed, and healthy.

Initially, I thought that the purpose of *Getting to Know You* was to benefit Africans alone because of my experience working in Africa, but as soon as I returned to Europe, I saw similar problems: lack of interest in marriage among men and women, and the number of marriages declining in churches, for the simple reason that people were no longer interested in marriage, or those who were married were no longer staying married. The promise "till death do us part" seemed irrelevant now. Even within the church, divorces and remarrying seemed to be the norm. I saw negligence on the part of the church in guiding would-be couples on the dos and don'ts before marriage. There was no serious attention paid to dating; partners were left to find out things on their own. The only time the church was involved was at the joining together, but at this stage there is little to nothing one can do or say to stop the love relationship.

I learnt to ask some questions about the people I ministered to who were in love relationships: How well do these two know each other? I mean, how well do they know each other in the eyes of God and not just the eyes of society?

How many times have we seen a relationship that looks perfect in the eyes of society, yet the marriage does not endure even for a year before the couple calls it quits?

I sincerely rejoice with you that you have found the bone of your bone and the flesh of your flesh and that you are preparing to spend the rest of your lives together. I would still ask you how well you know each other. It is very important to answer this question; the longevity of your marriage will depend on how well you know each other from start to finish. The notion that you will learn about your partner by marrying will not lead to an enduring relationship in the end.

I think there should be better preparation for marriage by getting to know each other beforehand. The goal of getting to know each other should bring you to the point of planning your wedding ceremony.

CHAPTER 3

Why Should I Get Married?

I have personally read several books on marriage, and after reading each one, I discovered there was still much I did not know about marriage. It's like the saying: marriage is one institution from which no one ever graduates. It is a continual school of learning until death do you part. I discovered an area we probably neglect or fail to pay enough attention to. We talk about dating, courtship, marriage itself, and living in a marriage, but we leave out a very vital aspect of planning towards marriage: how well the two people who are planning to marry know each other. We overlook this stage of courtship or consider it to be less important. So then the couple are left to themselves to figure out what they need to know about each other. They often talk about their good points: what makes them feel good about themselves, their career, their family background, and their success in sports or academics. You never hear daters talk about their weaknesses or bad habits. If the guy is a smoker and he knows his girlfriend does not like smoking, he may hide it from her or pretend that he has stopped. But later on, probably during the marriage, the bad habit will surface and create problems. It is important that those of us who are involved in the lives of two people like this offer them support before and during their preparation for marriage.

In many cases, a dispute arises between a couple when they have already said yes to each other or booked a venue for the wedding ceremony. I know of two people who called off their wedding four weeks after their engagement party because of irreconcilable differences. What was the problem? The bride-to-be complained that the marriage would not be ideal for her four-year-old son from a former relationship. She said the guy she had planned to marry was a heavy drinker. She also complained that he visited her apartment at very late hours of the night and then tried to spend the night in her apartment, using the excuse that it was too late for him to go home. She concluded that this man was not the type of man she wanted to have in the life of her young son. The guy, for his part, said that she was cheating on him with her ex-boyfriend, and that was why she did not want him around. I am sure that these two did not have enough time before their engagement to prepare for what marriage is about. The counselling session with their pastor, or whomever was entrusted with such responsibility, had not done a good job of preparing these two for what would be expected of them before they walked to the altar to say yes to each other. They had not dealt with their pasts, which would affect their future together. They had kept several things away from each other. It was wise that the young woman declined to go ahead with the marriage, even though it was painful and preparations were already in place.

Money doesn't compensate for happiness in marriage, nor for intimate knowledge of each other without sexual ideas. In a jovial competition meant for couples that took place in my local church years ago, wives were blindfolded, and each was asked to detect and recognize her husband through touching his nose only. Many of the couples had been married for years, yet most of them failed the test—the women each picked another man as their husband, and some could not recognize their spouses by scent. Why is such an insignificant thing like being able to recognize your spouse by feel or by scent so important for couples to know and practise? *Getting to Know You* will try to address this.

I write from the perspective of a Christian who believes in the full truth of the Bible, knowing there is a greater marriage to come that we also need to prepare for. Our physical marriage in the present is a clue to what Jesus Christ meant when he said he would come back for his church as a bride. He will be expecting a bride without blemish or crinkle. I will try not to twist the Word. I am going to make my facts as simple as possible so that everyone may understand. I have tried to use very clear biblical translations for reference in my writing, and I have spoken to more experienced people when it comes to marital matters so as to avoid unnecessary debate after reading the book.

Getting to Know You is in no way meant to contradict whatever has been written or will be written in the future on marriage. Rather, expect this book will complement all the other good books on marriage out there. I love marriage as an institution, I believe it is good, holy, and honourable to be in a marriage, an enjoyable one with all the blessings of God in it.

After all, it was written in the very beginning, "It is good." Those are not my words; they were spoken through the mouth of the Creator of heaven and earth and all that is in it. These words were intended to serve a purpose in the lives of God's creation. What could possibly not be good in God's creation? God himself provides us an answer in Genesis 2:18: "It is not good for the man to be alone. I will make a helper suitable for him."

Look at the sequence of events after that statement was made by God. The nature of God created man; the man probably didn't have feelings, but God himself saw that it was not good or complete for a man to live all by himself with all the other animals that God had created along with Adam.

Why didn't God find a helpmate for man among the animals? God had a better solution; he said, "I will make him a helper comparable to him and compactable to him. A helpmate that looks like him yet different."

> Then the Lord God made a woman from the rib he had taken out of the man and he brought her to the man. The man said, "This is now bone of my bones and flesh of my flesh; she shall be called 'woman' for she was taken out of man." (Genesis 2:22)

This event is what triggered the feeling for the opposite sex (in this case, the woman); anything outside this feeling for a woman is ungodly.

A man should and must have feeling for a woman. This is the plan of God for his people and his creation. Needless to say, some people are acting in contradiction to this God-given gift, seeking not to be alone by choosing to be with persons of the same sex or even with animals, which is against God's Word.

Now God's creation was "very good" (Genesis 1:31), and for this reason, a man shall leave his father and mother and be joined to his wife, and they shall become one flesh. Literally, God's Word is setting man free from the bond of his parents by asking him to leave (to establish his own home) with his wife. In today's society, parents want their son to marry, but he remains with them. No matter the wealth level of the family, let the man live with his wife where they can intimately become one without the interference of parents.

I want to believe that most people reading *Getting to Know You* are Christians who already have accepted the lordship of Jesus Christ as Lord and Saviour. If you have not, I am sure you are making the decision right now—the most important decision any person will ever make in life.

The second most important decision you will have to make is whom you plan to spend the rest of your life with as your spouse. So whether you are a man or a woman, you need to have such an ambition of whom you want to spend the rest of your life with.

I have heard people say, "But what if I choose not to marry?" Then I say to you, "You'll be missing a part of God's plan and purpose for your life as it was declared from the very beginning: that for this reason (i.e. marriage) shall a man leave his father and mother and cleave onto his wife, and the two shall become one. If Christ should come today, he will find you united with your spouse in holy marriage. If you choose not to marry, it is not a problem for God, but in such a case you should live a holy lifestyle and not lust after the same thing you say you do not want to have!

This decision of whom to choose to spend the rest of your life with will determine how you spend the rest of your life here on earth and will shape your future and ultimately your destiny. In fact, the decision of a life partner will determine the course of future generations, so it is important that you get this foundation-laying ceremony properly done, ensuring it is right and established in Jesus Christ.

I have no doubt in my mind that a godly marriage will withstand the storms of life and surpass them through the fulfilment that comes with marriage.

Again, yes, there are people who choose not to be married, for whatever reason. I respect this decision. And if they can live with it, no problem. But don't say you don't want to marry and yet in your heart lust for it. Then it becomes sin. And don't engage in sexual immoral behaviours which are against God's Word in order to satisfy your desire. If you cannot be like the apostle Paul, then, as he says, look for a partner and be married. It is no sin to desire to have a spouse.

Now, *Getting to Know You* will help you to prepare and give you tips for your children, your siblings, and your friends or those special people you know who have dreams of getting married one day.

First church marriage in Kenya with Cliffe Ombogo Oduor & Terry Millicent Abongó
Now Mr. & Mrs. Cliff Oduor

CHAPTER 4

Crossing Over

At what point in time do you start thinking of a subject of this nature like marriage? I guess that for a man, it mostly starts by his thinking of having a friendship that gradually blossoms into a union or relationship, so he finally decides to ask for the woman's hand in marriage, thereby establishing a marriage union. For some, it starts early, and for others it is a decision that comes much later in young adulthood. It doesn't matter when the decision is made; as long as you are not underage, that is too young to talk about marriage, you can think about it and choose it. One time a parent tell me that his thirteen-year-old son was in a serious relationship, I simply told him to stop joking. The guy was a kid; he did not know what he was saying. Marriage is not a joke; it's not something fun for a child to talk about. I made the decision to marry in my midthirties, but today much younger people are making the decision to get married much earlier. I don't think the problem has anything to do with age if you understand the essence of the decision you are making with your partner—but not at thirteen, please. I have given the idea of marriage much thought probably beginning when I was in my midtwenties, even though I knew I was not ready for marriage myself at that point. There was a time when I did seriously discuss this subject with an ex-girlfriend, but we waved it off because we probably thought it was too early and we were not ready yet. At least I wasn't. Things have changed so fast that I have seen young people getting married much younger. The youngest wedding I have witnessed was that of a twenty-one-year-old man wedding a nineteen-year-old woman. During my chat with them, I discovered that they didn't know much about each other apart from their college experience as students. It was love at first sight and nothing more. They did not consider each other's character or tolerance level, or the acceptance and pressure from peers, that often comes with a relationship eventually ending in a marriage.

If you are in a situation where you are getting to know someone who you think may be God's choice for you to marry and live with as a life partner, I want to bring to your attention to some basic important principles you must adhere to from the very beginning before you say yes to one another. I have researched these principles and have found them to be necessary if one is to have a good and lasting influence on one's relationships. I do not totally agree with the saying that "God shows my partner and me, and that's it." You need to know who your partner is and learn how to relate with her or him. What we had in the old days was just an "obey orders" arrangement where a woman was in an arranged marriage. She was handed over to a man as her husband, and she began to learn the man like a textbook while she was living in his house. It was just an "obeying orders" marriage most of the time; the woman had no say whatsoever in the marriage. The man determined everything for the woman in the marriage. In many cases, such marriages do not work out. But the women endured such an arrangement all for the sake of their families and children.

The principles I am writing about in *Getting to Know You* must be followed to the letter. If you take that advice, then you will be glad you did. You can share this information with your pastor or whoever is counselling you. Use it as a guide sheet in preparation for your wedding.

The First Principle Is to Trust in God

From the very beginning, trust in God totally for your relationship. Even in the choice you make, trust the Lord with it. Seek his guidance and direction for your future. Continue to surrender to God's will; learn not to manipulate, deceive, or lie in order to get your will done. I suggest you hold the relationship in an open hand, saying, "Not my will but your will be done." Add, "Not my time but God's time" and "Not my way but his way", especially when it comes to the decision of marriage. Trust him all the way. I have spoken to so many people whose marriages had endured through the turbulent crises of married life. The honest truth of why their marriages survived is that they held on to their trust in God. Although many of them did not start with trusting God, when they came to understand the truth, they turned their lives and their marriages over to God, at which point he became the centre of their lives and marriages.

The Second Principle Is to Stay in the Light

From the very beginning, when you find the man or woman whom you like or are thinking seriously about, do not hide him or her away from the people who are most important to you, particularly your spiritual guardians, meaning your pastor and his (or her) wife. Communicate about the relationship from the beginning with these people who are over you and around you. Parents, pastors, and home group leaders within your church need to know what is happening in your life. In many settings, you are advised against marrying because you are not sure of the relationship yet. Well, a relationship is not a gamble. It is not a Ferrari test-drive where you do away with one car to test-drive another, and if the one you're trying out is not good or suitable for you, you return it to the showroom. A relationship is something deeper. You need to think it through and be convinced from the beginning that you want it, you are ready for it, and you want to go for it. We need to discourage the idea of a relationship as something that you try first, and if it does not fit or work, then you abandon it and go for another one. Many people have gone into a relationship with this mentality or with the intention to test-run it and then get out of it if it does not work out, but today people who think this way are stuck in relationships because of a wrong choice they made, like sleeping with one another after first meeting, resulting in the woman's getting pregnant and the couple's then having a child together. For that reason alone, the two people decided to develop the relationship into a marriage. When you go into a marriage this way, it may work or may not work, but it is not the best approach. Therefore, it is not advisable to do things that way.

The Third Principle Is to Live in Purity

You must resolve from the very beginning not to do anything that would contaminate you or your partner in the eyes of God and also in the eyes of people. Purity is defined as being in the state of unsullied by sin or moral wrong, lacking knowledge of evil. I personally advise that you should make sure that you don't have any form of physical contact with your partner. Avoid such closeness as facial kissing, hugging, or talking about sexual subjects, which could arouse the wrong feelings in an emotional manner or even bring about marriage prematurely. One of the wrong teachings popular today is that once two people declare an interest in each other, they may hug, kiss, and even live together. This is wrong, however. It exposes the two people to emotional danger and to the danger of committing sexual sin. Sex is totally a taboo at this stage and should not be a subject of discussion in the relationship.

The Fourth Principle Is to Remain Above Reproach

Recently, I was discussing this subject of being above reproach with two persons who were preparing for marriage. They found it strange because they thought once they had gotten engaged, they were already semimarried and could do whatever they wished to do. I told them that was wrong. "Not until you are fully wedded; you are still not married." I told them that because of this, they needed to remain above reproach. You need to avoid doing anything that might cause you to be accused of committing a fault, doing something shameful, or brining disgrace upon yourself or your partner. It is nothing special these days to see a woman heavily pregnant in her wedding gown walking down the aisle for a wedding ceremony. Is this not a mockery of marriage for those of us who have done what we have been expected to do, waiting anxiously for our wedding night after we were pronounced husband and wife? It is even more common these days that there is already a child or children before marriage is even talked about. I am well informed that in some cultures, it is expected to test the woman's fertility in advance, meaning that the woman must first become pregnant before wedding. Even some churches are subscribing into this idea and are twisting the rules to accommodate marrying women who are already pregnant. Churches do this because they feel they have to please the people. To avoid such situations, I advise young couples to spend less time together alone in private environs, such as being alone together in each other's house. I remember in my adolescence when girls started visiting my home. My parents insisted that for no reason should we be in the bedroom alone or even in the sitting room alone. There was a lot of supervision of the relationship from both families. There were a lot of regulations on the relationship. We didn't enjoy it, but it was helpful to keep us out of trouble. The same was applicable when I visited the girl's house; we were not allowed to stay alone in private spaces.

Some people find this teaching strange. They argue that we have to adjust to current trends and modernization. But I beg to differ. I say, let us teach our younger generation the right things to do. It is proven that young people find it difficult to abstain from sexual sin when they are left alone. Which is better to do, be among people and avoid sexual sin, or be alone and sin—even though many people don't see it as sinning? What I have learnt over the years is that all that we hurry to do in courtship, such as having sex, being close, kissing, and hugging, we may enjoy it as much as we want as soon as we say yes to one another. The idea of feeling that you are not mature or macho enough because you remain a virgin before your wedding is wrong. You have preserved yourself for your bride or groom, and you can enjoy your relationship together. You should be very proud of yourself and of your partner. The Bible recommends this. In biblical times, it was a joyous ceremony when the bride was found to be a virgin. It was a source of great pride to her and her family.

The Fifth Principle Is to Live without Hypocrisy

As the friendship grows, your pastor and the other leaders of your church should know about it. Then your home group or the Bible study leader within your church should be told. This enables a young man and a young woman to get to know each other in real-life situations rather than in the artificial atmosphere of one-on-one dates, with such people pretending not to know each other when in church by sitting separately or far apart! Telling others about your relationship also helps to keep the relationship pure and above reproach because you know people are aware and are watching you. Many young people in relationships are in denial, playing holy in church and fooling around outside of church. When confronted, they deny what they're doing, saying "We are just friends, discussing school subjects, doing sports together"—and every other lie in the book. Come clean. It will help shape the relationship and set it on a good course, if it is going to blossom into the type of relationship you will be proud of in the future.

The Sixth Principle Is to Live with Understanding

I have seen terrible crimes committed in marriage, for instance spousal abuse, both physical and emotional, and I just wonder, *Why did you marry this person if you hate him [or her] so much?* The principle of being "unequally yoked" should guide us in our marriage decision. Listen, you need to understand that if you marry a person who abused you when you were dating, you cannot expect that he or she will change overnight and become loving and caring. My suggestion that you wed a Christian brother or sister is based on the idea that you will get to know each other better; in the eyes of God you are one family, bonded together as one person in faith and belief. We must at all times have this understanding in our relationships with one another.

I witnessed abuse in a marriage relationship at a young age when I was in college. A couple lived opposite my hostel, and several times I had intervene to separate them during a fight. In fact, I had to rescue the woman from the beating of her husband. The man was a banker, the wife a nurse, and they were married with their wedding photos on display in their sitting room. They had two beautiful daughters. From afar, they looked a family couple, but they fought nearly every weekend in the presence of those two innocent girls. The husband and the wife worked in two different cities, but from Friday evening to Monday morning, when the husband was back at home, it was always one form of quarrel or another. They got so loud and violent that we students living opposite their house had to intervene on many occasions. At one point, I became physical with the husband and warned him to stop beating his wife. I said that if he was tired of the marriage, he should just walk out instead of battering his wife. Years later, I saw the woman, and she told me the marriage had ended. She could not take it any longer. The abuse had continued and even became more aggressive. He had taken to drinking, and he beat her all the more, threatening to kill her. She left him and later got married to an ex-boyfriend from college whom she had loved. She had chosen the other man over the one she loved because her family felt that he, a banker, was in a better position to take care of her. The relationship did not work out as expected. She had vowed never to marry again. In her words, "I didn't know him. He was so nice and kind to me during the short time we were dating. He always brought me gifts, and he was polite to members of my family. They were convinced." For years, nobody believed her story of her abuse, until they saw her bruises all over her body. There was no understanding in the marriage. And despite the fact that there was a problem, the husband was not willing to work on it.

This woman's second marriage is doing very well. She is happy now with her daughters. Her ex-husband is still fighting his addiction to alcohol, which cost him his esteemed job at the bank.

The Seventh Is Principle Is to Live in Obedience

The union you are aiming to establish should be one of obedience to the command to expand God's kingdom here on earth. You must understand that the relationship you intend to establish will help to further the kingdom of God. It is not about you or me but about Jesus Christ, the author of marriage. "But seek first the kingdom of God and his righteousness, and all these things will be added to you" (Matthew 6:33). Marriage is one of those things that will be added to you. Therefore, when you are starting a relationship, have it in the back of your mind that it is in accordance with God's will and command. My daughter understands that she does not have to be in a relationship to please her mother or me; rather, her relationship is to please God. With that understanding in mind, she enjoys our support.

The Eighth Principle Is to Live in Freedom

When all is done in God's counsel, in the light, and under authority as I have suggested, there is freedom to get to know each other without worrying about what people will say or what they are thinking. Don't worry about gossip or rumours of being too holy. Such gossip cannot survive when exposed to the light. Therefore, stay focused on these basic principles as a starting point of your relationship. Make yourself a promise that you will do your best to keep, follow, and obey these principles in your quest to get to know each other better and possibly move into a relationship that would lead you to wedding and establishing a marriage.

Tony Omondi Alaka & Emma Magwaro, now Mr. & Mrs. Anthony Alaka

CHAPTER 5

Your Dating

Now that we have discussed the first step, it is time to talk about making your decision about whom to date or go out with. Put in common person's language, it's now time to focus on when, how, and where dating starts. When you find the person your heart longs for or desires, you are expected to start talking to your pastor or church counsellor, or another trusted person, preferably a married couple, for tips on advancing a good relationship.

A lot of things have changed since the time I had my first date with my wife. Now I am a pastor who often has to deal with men and women who are in relationship. In my case, once I spotted the woman I eventually married, I prayed about her and she constantly remained on my mind. I spoke first with my assistant pastor at the time, Felix Asare, asking for his advice, and he asked me to pray even more about her. After a few months, I returned to him, and he asked me to speak to her then. This is how Sandra and I made our first contact. Later, a relationship developed. The rest is now history. She has been married to me for over twenty years.

The mention of dating, to some Christians sounds like sexual compromise.

Many can't recollect their dating experience, and many don't recall thinking that it was very important to the build-up of their relationship. The mention of dating, for some Christians, sounds likes permission to entertain sexual thoughts. How will you develop a relationship if there is no dating? Dating is a chance to get to know each other better, apart from seeing each other in church. Have you gone out together on a dinner date, a movie date, or a relaxing picnic date with other friends? In my time, we had singles' fellowship in the church for all young men and women who were yet to be married to participate in. It was not a dating fellowship. Our leaders never encouraged it, but it exposed young men and women to the good time to be had in fellowship. We participants shared good times together in fellowship over a meal, a drink, or sports and through activities like Bible study, going on picnics, doing sporting activities, staging dramas, and engaging in quiz competitions. In this way, we got to know each other better. These activities were supervised by the youth leaders of the church. It created avenue for unmarried young people to interact and get to know each other better as brothers and sisters in the church.

Years later, some did find their spouses from this type of fellowship in the church. How great that is. Most of those marriages are our examples to learn from today. Even though my wife was part of this fellowship group, I didn't even know her name until after nearly two years of being together in the same fellowship group and the same Bible study group in the church. So strict was the discipline, that the best I could do was to say to her, "God bless you, sister." I just knew her as a sister in the church. I also knew she was a nurse because she sometimes came to the Bible study in her work uniform. There was nothing more to our "relationship" than that.

The pastor did not object when I told him of my interest in Sandra. Instead, he encouraged me to pray first, keep it open, pray about it again, and keep him apprised.

When I started giving serious thought to having a wife, the Lord brought Sandra to my attention. My first reaction was, *No. I know her, and she knows me. What will she say, and what will other people say?* Probably this is what I had been on my mind for the past two years. I struggled with what people would say rather than what I felt about her or what she would say to me. However, I was able to overcome that once I'd spoken with one of my trusted friends about my intention to talk to a woman in the church. He did not object. He asked me to pray first, keep the line of communication open, pray about it again, and keep him informed. Once I'd spoke to Sandra and asked for her friendship, even though she was a young Christian woman, she did not get overexcited. She did not show any emotion. Rather, she calmly told me, "I will think about it." She requested more time to pray about it. Listen, this was just a request for friendship.

How can he profess to love you, this person who knows hardly anything about you?

Some start talking of love using all the jargon of the day. Once a young woman told me, speaking of the young man she was interested in, "He says he loves me." How can he love you, a person you hardly know? What I first noticed in my talk with the young woman who would later become my wife was that we had something in common—the idea to pray about our friendship. And that is exactly what we did. Praying about it means seeking wise counsel from God on the journey one is about to embark on.

After confirmation, Sandra and I went out on few occasions as permitted by our pastor. We enjoyed an evening outing for dinner with two other friends, a walk in the park, a visit to her family members, and a visit to her place of work on her invitation. We met several times at the bus station, where I waited for her to return from her job. We would chat for a few minutes while everyone else went ahead to their respective destinations. We spoke a few times on telephone. There were no mobile phones then, so I made use of public phones to call her when she was free from her job. She could not visit me since I lived alone, except on my birthday, when more people were at my house. I remember going to watch a football game with her at Ajax Stadium; it was fun getting to know each other better. After those quality times together, it was obvious that we had started developing stronger feelings for each other. I lived in a one-room apartment.

She only visited the house when I was not there. Only once did she visit me in my apartment, for my thirty-sixth birthday celebration. I still remember that visit. She came early to drop off a bouquet of flowers she had bought for my birthday celebration. She left for her job, to return later in the afternoon. But when my Dutch friends and other guests came to celebrate with me in my apartment, interestingly, she had left the apartment, leaving the flowers behind. Everyone who had come to visit me admired the flowers. In fact, they told me that the person who had brought the flowers must be in love with me. A poor African boy, I was not used to flowers. I didn't even get the message that she was sending along with the flowers. I took a memorable photograph of that bouquet of flowers, which I have kept up to this day.

Sandra had a bigger apartment, living by herself, where I could have held the party, but I chose to have it in my own apartment. It was an event not to impress but to celebrate with my friends. Also, members of Sandra's family had advised her, asking why we didn't move in together if we were so much in love with each other as we claimed. We declined that temptation and that option; we knew it was not right, so we didn't do it. When we look back, we say that we enjoyed every moment of our dating. It was not boring. We did our best not to sin with our bodies while we worked towards our wedding. The argument young people today put up is that they have more life experience and probably will have no way to experiment again at age thirty-six. I have worked with young people who started dating early, grooming them to stay pure, clean, and holy and to wait for the appointed time. Some of those young men and women are married today and are enjoying their marriages.

I recommend a period of dating. I would not put a time frame on how long the period of dating should be. It could last anywhere from a year to as long as you want it to last, but again, the underlining objective of dating is to get to know each other better without sinning.

Dating can be the most pleasant period in a sound relationship.

Dating is the most pleasant period of talking and talking and talking, never getting tired of talking to each other, and of sharing your experiences, expectations, dreams, visions, and insight, even your past and your purpose, with one another.

Avoid keeping secrets during your period of dating. Don't encourage secret admirers, who may make you begin to behave suspiciously sometimes in your relationship. Again, be open to one another and keep it real from the very beginning. I told my girlfriend then about my past involvement with women and the relationships that I'd kept; I talked about those relationships that still brought painful memories and those young women I'd dated who had moved on and yet we remained friends. I am an African. My girlfriend was from South America, and her background was Dutch, and she was ready and open for a sincere and honest truthful relationship. Even some friends told me that I had revealed too much to her, but I assured them that the relationship was open and honest and that we were sincere with each other. Sandra had her own personal experiences too, which she shared with me. So when an ex-boyfriend tried to harass her, he was surprised at the support I gave her, and he backed off.

There was so much Sandra didn't know about Africans. I was her source of information, and I provided clarification vis-à-vis misinformation she had picked from the roadside and from members of her family. There was the notion that Africans in Holland were lazy drug peddlers or fraudsters. As much as there was truth to this generalization, I was different. Sandra needed to know that. Within our period of dating, she saw the real me. She defended my person even when I was not there, saying that I was just different from what other people knew about, or what experiences they had had with, Africans.

Friends warned me that I was giving too much information away and that Sandra could use it against me if things did not go well with our relationship. But the opposite has been my experience. She has helped me to deal with my past, has supported me in my present decision-making, and has worked with me as we've moved into our future. In fact, if I had not been totally open with her, I would have gotten into trouble with her much earlier in our marriage. Everything I'd told her about my family life, she could confirm during our first visit to my homeland, Nigeria. I showed her everything she needed to see and told her everything she needed to know about my family. I took her to my place of birth, my origin, where she met with my parents and siblings. She was then able to verify almost all the things I had told her since the beginning. Of course that made her more confident in the relationship. She had been told that many African men had secret wives back in Africa before coming abroad. I didn't. And if I had, I would have informed her. She knew I had no second wife anywhere else in the world. She is the one and only wife I have.

The longer dating takes, the greater the danger of other issues coming up: How long will it take for him or her to make the decision? When will he ask the million-dollar question "Will you marry me?" For me it took just over a year from when we officially expressed our feeling towards each other to my proposing marriage to Sandra.

After one year of dating, I was sure, without the shadow of a doubt, that she was the woman I wanted to spend the rest of my life with as long as God gave me life. I had known her for nearly two years before I proposed to her, so that was approximately a three-year period of watching, thinking, praying before acting upon my desire to marry her.

If you have a good dating relationship, it will actually help you determine more quickly the time when you will propose to the woman you're seeing. So take the dating period more seriously and use it to get to know each other better.

I would not recommend online dating for sincere and sound Christians.

The dating I recommend in *Getting to Know You* is not the same as dating through the Internet or visiting dating websites or dating clubs and what have you. I have also seen Christian institutions starting dating blogs and websites, and I see Christian men and women filling out the forms and paying money to register for such websites.

I know some who have made a journey of thousands of miles, travelling to see the person they'd met through such a website, and they've mostly returned disappointed. A woman I know travelled from Holland to Australia to meet a guy she had met through a dating website, supposedly a Christian website. She came back disappointed. Her intention was to stay in a hotel while she and the man made appointments or went out on dates, but the man already wanted her in his bed. And when she objected, he became hostile and, in fact, threatened her. He stopped being kind to her and even stopped communicating with her before she left his country to return to Holland. It was a terrible experience that ended the communication. I wonder, if face-to-face contact is not effective, how much more difficult is it to communicate well with someone you meet online, with only pictures to show you how nice they are, when in reality the person is a totally strange character?

I wonder, if face-to-face contact is not effective, then how can online dating suffice with only pictures to see?

I do not recommend that a sincere and honest Christian subscribe to online dating, which I see as a "try your luck" measure. Well, dating is not try your luck. You work on it, and if you do it with honesty, you will get a positive result from it.

Dating should be worked on and should be accompanied by honesty. If so, then one will realize a splendid result from it.

Pastor Kevin Omondi Owino & Elizabeth Odera, now Pastor & Pastor Mrs Kevin Omondi

CHAPTER 6

Training for Singles (Men and Women)

In the past several generations, the Christian church has gradually adopted the world's ways where it comes to how marriage should be taught in the church, particularly to young men and women. The church might call itself evangelical or Pentecostal, but it has in fact departed from some of the most basic Christian truths found in God's Word. We hardly hear teachings on courtship, dating, weddings, or marriage. Rather, it is all about prosperity and materialism. Young men are working very hard to have prosperity and gather material things before they think of marriage, and they think their material accumulations will bring them a woman with whom they may live a happy married life thereafter. This is not true. Many families are suffering because, even with their wealth, they have left broken homes and broken children in their wake. Christian families are breaking apart and marriages are breaking down, and we wonder why. Our young people are not educated about healthy, godly relationships before they enter into marriage. Marriage has become a fashion trend; if this one doesn't fit you, then take it off and go get another. We are living in a denial, denying the truth of the Word of God.

God has clearly taught us through his Bible about marriage. God has ordained marriage and has left the responsibility to us to teach it to our children. Marriage builds a home and creates stability for children to be raised in the proper way. Many children have struggled because of a broken home, which is a result of a broken marriage or possibly not even a marriage but living together or engaging in extramarital sexual activity. People may make excuses for themselves, but it doesn't matter, because in the end they will still suffer the same consequences as the world, and perhaps even worse. We need to stand up and defend what God has given to us, namely the institution of marriage. We need to safeguard it. And how do we do that except by teaching our young people the value of being married and staying married?

Marriage is not outdated, not old-fashioned or irrelevant; all the substitutions are irrelevant. There is no substitute for marriage. Therefore, is it important that we teach it to our children and safeguard it, so we can still have healthy marriages. God graciously has given wisdom to the writers of the Bible. Sixty-six books were written to give us the moral code contained in the Bible.

God has also given us minds to interpret those words. He allows us to learn how to live a great life. The secret is in the Word of God.

Marriage builds a home and creates stability for children to be raised in the proper way.

Let us not be deceived: things are not going to get better or change by themselves. Christians are not in any way protected from the attacks of secularism or the tricks of the devil to destroy a marriage. If you observe carefully, you will see that many young men and women are no longer interested in marriage; they want to have children, but they're not willing to provide them a home where there is a father and a mother. In a marriage, you first create a home before having children. You will build the family through your home, and right now the value of the family and the home system is being destroyed. We need to know God's Word and resolve to keep true to everything that is in it for us, and that includes our marriage. I decided to do this over twenty years ago, and my wife and I still have a marriage today; God is protecting it for us as we work on it.

Most people will get married one day. Now is the time to become pure in thought and action so that you may be guided against any form of sexual abuse of your body before you are married. People today need to learn what they need to do to put away those things that are fun, as it is called in today's society. I am told that we live in a generation where it is no longer possible to find a virgin. I do not believe this assertion. There are still virgins among our youths, and they are preserving themselves for their future spouses. I salute these young men and women. I say, stay firm and remain committed to God in your decision.

Young men and women should approach maturity at around twelve or thirteen years old. I am told that for girls, it even starts much earlier now, so this means that teaching and training on the subject of sex and marriage needs to start much earlier than ever before. Girls should be told the dangers of wrongly exposing their bodies to the opposite sex and the consequences for such silly actions. Do not think that you cannot train to become a good husband or wife, and don't think that you're too young to hear about marriage. Also, don't wait until you are about to be married to learn. Then it is too late to correct the wrong impression that you do not need training before marriage. Our lusts and self-oriented sinful natures wage war against what is right, good, and lovely. This is why God commanded man to leave his father and mother and be joined to his wife. This is a special divine love that comes from God, so that human beings do not behave like an animals, sleeping with each other with reckless abandon.

Discussing Marriage with Singles

Sometimes it is hard for singles to talk about marriage. Singles, however, adopt attitudes early on that will affect their marriages. Unfortunately, most of these learned attitudes are not good. Who can tell me what is wrong with the marriages they see in the movies they watch? Many people don't even see the flaws, so they're not disgusted enough by the movies not to watch them. People must deliberately think about marriage in order to have a good marriage. I have challenged everyone, whether married or not, to seriously contemplate whether the world's ideas have influenced their thinking, their expectations, and their perspectives on marriage. But don't miss the most important part: God is the owner of marriage, and his ways for marriage are our guiding tools for marriage.

Do you believe that obedience to God's Word will result in a good marriage and a good family and that disobedience results in bad marriages and bad families? If so, then discuss what it takes to have a good marriage. But start where God starts. Let us emphasize the things God has emphasized. Marriage is special and wonderful, but it takes a commitment to obeying God's Word if it is to be successful. Several training exercises for both single men and single women should be given. If such a thing is not possible, then one needs to understand what the implications of the truth are (read John 8:32). There is no hope for improvement until one understands truth.

> **God is the owner of marriage, and his ways for marriage are our guiding tools for marriage.**

It is helpful for people to share how their pastors, church counsellors, and parents trained them for marriage. Neglect of proper training is still training; it's just very poor training in that you take whatever you see on television or in movies as being ideal for your marriage. But it is not ideal. As one remembers his or her days growing up, it helps the individual to isolate the particular problems he or she will face. For instance, I learnt how to cook while living with my parents. Today in my marriage, I am able to complement my wife in cooking. Sometimes in the home, I do household activities, which some men find it difficult to do after I tell them to do these things during our counselling sessions. People learn from their parents in two ways: by observing (1) parent–child relationships and (2) father–mother interactions.

A person's marriage will never *naturally* be better than that of his or her parents. That is why marriages tend to go from poor to worse—because many people are operating under that misapprehension. Only by identifying where one has accepted faulty perspectives, and by accepting God's grace and truth to make real life changes, can a great marriage be obtained.

Remember that it is best to discuss some topics among either all women or all men (rather than in a mixed group). Either split up for discussing those topics or don't discuss them at all. The talk will be much more fruitful if you address the men and women separately.

My Experience with Single Men and Women

I dealt mostly with young men and women who were living together, and a few who were yet unmarried, in our church in Kenya. Our church was made up of 60 per cent to 70 per cent youths, young men and women under the age of thirty. I know for sure that many of them desired to marry in the future. So I thought that writing a book to encourage these young people was necessary. It is important that they know they should not make the same mistakes as their parents. They should put away all the fun associated with dating or courtship, as many of them think it is a game or the fashion of their peer group to have a girlfriend or boyfriend. They figure that after a period of fooling with their bodies, they may now dedicate their bodies to the Lord. God is not for leftover or used-up youths; he wants pure young men and women for his honour and glory.

23

Young men should be taught to put away childishness. They should be taught the best way to be good husband material, taking their examples from the home and the church. Many youth think they do not need training before marriage. This is another lie which has been used to fool young people. As Christians, we need to begin early in training our young men to know that dating a woman should lead to marriage and nothing more or nothing less; they have to learn to deal with their lusts and the sinful desires of human nature for this very reason. We should begin to train the boys and girls on keeping their minds and bodies pure so that they are not contaminated before they come of age. In Western societies, I see kids saying they are in love. I wonder what they understand of love. To them, it is just affection for the opposite sex, or admiration at most. They need to be taught to train their bodies to be disciplined and to engage in sacrificial service. There is a war going on between the flesh and the Spirit of God; the flesh desires things that the Spirit does not yet approve. The church has to take responsibility to teach its young people to fight and wage the war against the flesh in their lives. If I should put the question to you right now as a single man or woman, what would you say is the kind of man or woman you want to marry someday? You will give me a long list of great qualities you desire from a marriage partner. Where did you learn those values?

Did you learn them in a clubhouse? On a dance floor? In a beer joint or café? Definitely not! You probably thought of a church or a wedding ceremony where everyone looked his or her best. In the old days, men looked to the homes of the women they found interesting. Why? They thought that the woman had learnt the values of being a woman from her parents, particularly from her mother. You are wise if you search for such a woman, because as the Bible recommends in Proverbs 21:9, "It is better to live in a corner of a roof than in a house shared with a contentious woman."

The woman is expected to have cultivated a genuine skill to satisfy her husband once she marries. She has already learnt how to cook and how to take care of a home; she does not learn to do these things when she gets to the husband's house, or else she would have problems. A single man is also expected to have learnt how to be a man who can love his wife and provide for her needs.

There are new trends in society which are affecting marriages. This is all the more reason why we need to teach these things to our young singles. There is the idea of feminism, which advocates for women's equality with men, or even women's superiority to men. Therefore, the idea of a wife, according to such feminists, is someone who is inferior and abused, which the feminists claim is something that women should resist. It is a wrong notion and a deception, one which is affecting many young women who are not able to marry or stay in a marriage. We have to see marriage from the perspective of God. Women are precious in the sight of God. He created woman and designed her to enjoy marriage. He knows how best a woman may fulfil her God-given role as a helpmate to her husband. Obviously a woman must be married to fulfil this role. A woman fulfils a role that no other creature, including another man, can fulfil, and that is to bring forth life. Only a woman is charged to do that by God.

Many single women are being taught to retain their individual rights and opinions when they enter a marriage, but I can tell you that this does not work. It is better for such women not to marry than to marry and then refuse to submit to their husbands. Such a woman will live in a miserable marriage and be unhappy. Marriage is not a competition between a man and a woman. The man is charged with his responsibilities as the woman is charged with her responsibilities, and the two need to work together as a team to have a good marriage, the two of them becoming one.

God has fortunately not just made two people and then called them to work together the best they can. This is all homosexuals can do. No, God has a much better plan. When he designed man and woman, he fully integrated into their beings, physical, emotional, and otherwise, the ability to blend as one in the context of marriage and produce children in a like manner.

It is absolutely foolish for a man to want to be like a woman or for a woman to want to be like a man because they envy the opposite role. As long as one envies the other's role, one will never be content or focused on his or her own responsibilities. A body does not need two left hands! A marriage does not need two heads! Because there is a union, a perfect blending of two people into one, there can only be one leader. God has called the man to be the head and the wife to submit. Because of sin, however, there are two competing, or we could call them worldly, approaches.

Parents, train your boys and girls. The church should complement this training with further training, teaching young people how to be a husband or a wife. We teach them to be successful in their academics and in sports, so why do we not give them home training to be a good husband or a submissive wife? We should avoid training them with the ungodly value of making a lot of money and hiring extra hands to cook, wash, babysit, and run errands. What happens when your husband gets used to the meals prepared by your housemaid? What happens when his compliments about the good cooking are not for you as the wife but for your house help? A good wife should prepare her husband meals—the way to a man's heart is through his stomach, an old adage says—but if you don't cook for him, then the person who does so will get into his heart.

The world is teaching us to stay focused on looking beautiful and acting clever. I say that taking good care of your home is the best treasure you can bring into your young marriage. Pay attention to how your parents are living now that you are still at home; the best gift your parents can give you is to teach you good things before you step out to get married as a man or a woman.

In the home, you should learn how to happily serve others; otherwise, you will not be able to cope with your husband, with any others who may come to live with you, and of course your own children once you have them. When I served in Africa, my church wanted to get me house help, but I refused the offer. Together with my wife, we took care of our two daughters. We did our shopping, cooking, and washing, and we lived together, as a family. Many were pleasantly surprised to see how we lived despite our having come from Europe. One Saturday morning, some of my churchmen visited my home and found me washing my wife's and children's clothes. They looked at me with shock and surprise, asking me, "How is it that a pastor is washing his wife's clothes and those of his children?"

I laughed before responding, "First I am a husband and a father before being a pastor." I taught them, "These are the things that will help you to build a happy home for yourself and to have a blessed marriage."

A man needs to understand a woman. She is made differently. Just focus on what God told us to do: "Love your wives as yourself." Your wife will go through special emotional ups and downs. Just keep steady in your love, and you will see that your wife will better respond to your leadership. Be insensitive, and it will be hard for you; if you don't understand a woman's nature, you will find it difficult to study her in your marriage situation with all the changes that will come. With training, you are step ahead. At least you are prepared for what to expect.

Similarly, the woman needs to understand the man when he tries to exercise spiritual leadership in the home. God has given him that responsibility to lead his home as the husband, father, and priest. Some women struggle with that, particularly those who claim they are called as church leaders with titles. It does not matter which anointing you have or what title you carry; your husband remains the head of the family and of the home and should be accorded that respect and honour. He has been trained to lead his home.

When you as a man pray with your wife, find out what her special needs are. Spend time each day talking together, praying together, and planning the family together. She will become your spiritual companion and helpmate. I don't think this type of home will suffer any problems. God will stand with such a couple and fight for them, and there will be no room for the devil to gain a foothold into this family.

One of the challenges I have noticed among young people relates to the question of unconditional love. *Can I love her forever?* Yes you can. The singles need to be taught to set their minds and their focus on affectional love for each other, which can only come from the love of God. Jesus Christ loved us first and unconditionally, the same type of love he wants to see in a marriage. Call it blind love, but in any event, love each other intensely. Just trust God that your love for each other will pay off.

A writer wrote, "What do you think God is going to ask you when you get to heaven? 'Did you love your wife [or your husband]?' Do you think you will be able to tell the Lord the excuses, 'I didn't know what I was getting into when I married her' or 'If I had a wife like [so-and-so's], then …' or 'I was too busy with my …' or 'I just was trying to get my own life together'? None of these excuses will cut it. Husbands are to unconditionally love their wives."

The point in all of this is to establish a context of love where the tenderness, love, and glory of the two can appear. You cannot fake love; it is either that you are in love or you're not. This is not a question that you ask each other! "Do you still love me?" Why do you want to marry someone if you are not sure you love each other? Your love for each other should be above every other thing, including the love you have for yourself, if such a thing is possible. After all, you are becoming one. When the wife is happy, the husband is happy, and when she is sad, he is sad. This must be established during the relationship: you must persistently treat each other nicely and remain in love because God cares about you and your partner.

The point in all of this is to establish a context of love where the tenderness, love, and glory of the two people in love can appear. You cannot fake love; it is either you are in love or you're not.

I summarize by saying that the world is absolutely wrong when they say that we don't need to teach our young men and women how to be a husband and a wife respectively, even saying that young people have a choice not to be married. The world says this, but it is largely because they are rebellious towards the Word of God and towards marriage, which he instituted, and want to make it look like a fun affair. It is not, and it will never be so. The sanctity of human life is in a marriage; children should be raised up within such an environment if we wish to have a better society. Therefore, parents, don't deny your children the opportunity to learn how to be a husband or a wife, starting in the home and taking whatever the church is able to contribute. Young people have nothing to learn from a society that is destroying marriages.

Instead of trying to think that society is better off, the parents ought to simply focus on what God has designed for the family and then do their best in training their children, not only with education but also with the norms and morals required for a person to be a good man or a good woman in society in general.

Those of us who are successful in our marriages should offer counsel to the singles, both men and women, and not proudly, because it is not our doing but is God who enables us to live together in harmony and love. Let us continue to shine the values of marriage and to teach that it is possible for husband and wife to live together in peace and to take on the responsibilities assigned to them as husband and wife.

Their calling in marriage is for the man to be the head of the household and for the wife to submit. It is through this special calling that they can become one and live out a great marriage. Because of sin, the man needs to specially focus on unconditionally loving his wife. The part of the wife is critical in the whole plan of God for the salvation of humankind. Christ used submissiveness to accomplish what authority and power is not able to accomplish in our society today. The wife needs to value her role and not despise it and to raise her children in like manner.

Those of us who are successful in our marriages should offer counsel to the singles, both men and women, not proudly, because it is not our doing but the doing of God, who enables us to live together in harmony and love.

From left is Pastor & Mrs. Iruh, the couple in the middle and Dr.
Rev & Mrs. George Kennedy of Dominion Chapel
Dr Kevin Omamo Ndai & Carolyne Adienge, now Dr. & Mrs Kevin Omamo Ndai

CHAPTER 7

Talking of Marriage

The purpose of this chapter is to help you understand the process of change that needs to take place before wedding. If your dating goes fine, it is important to return to your pastor or guardian for an update instead of assuming that you will inform him or her when you have decided or are ready to move on to the next stage or plan of action, which necessarily would be a wedding plan. Remember, I started by informing my confidant, my assistant pastor, of my love affair, and he asked me to give him feedback.

Never forget those crucial talks or appointments. You may get carried away with the fun and joy because things are developing well, but remember that the relationship needs to stay on course. I returned to my pastor and told him of the progress of my relationship. He then suggested that it was time to inform my senior pastor of what was happening. He made an appointment for us to see our senior pastor then, Pastor Jofrey Leito, who gave me an audience first and later asked me to come back with my fiancée, Sandra. We told him what had been happening. He listened very carefully, and he asked us very private questions, such as if we were living together and if we had already had sexual contact. The answers were no. He advised us to remain faithful so that we could enjoy the blessings of God over our relationship.

Pastor Leito told me and Sandra that he would hand us off to one of the pastors of the church for marital counselling. Even though we had not yet decided to get married, we had expressed our intention to consider that step as soon as we had properly informed our families.

Sandra and I were privileged to have been counselled by two pastors, the first one for about six months and the second one for another four months leading up to our wedding. Pastor Robby and Eline Wiebers led the counselling session, which involved our visiting their homes twice a week, taking a Saturday outing, and having a short meeting after church service. It was a commitment from both of us to be guided in the journey of life that we intended to embark upon.

We enjoyed the experiences of these pastors, who were married, who were very senior to us in age, and who had longevity in their marriages. Those counselling sessions gave us things to talk about when we met privately, such as where we planned to live after our wedding, the number of children we planned to have in the marriage, God willing, our relationship with both our families, and our walk with God together.

We were allowed to ask any kind of question, whatever was weighing on our minds either individually or collectively, and we were given satisfactory answers. I thought I knew so much about marriage in those ten months of counselling. Once a month, we met with our senior pastor to share our experiences with him.

It was a commitment from both of us to be helped and guided in this crucial stage of life.

The next step was getting to know my fiancée's family better: her brothers and sisters, close family relatives, and some extended family members whom she was in contact with. Probably it was a bit complex because she no longer had biological parents; her brothers and sisters were her guardians. I seemed to get on well with the sisters, who really didn't object to our relationship, but it was a different story with the brothers, one of whom was sceptical for obvious reasons, namely that I was a Nigerian. He had met some Nigerians in a Dutch prison who were involved in all sorts of crimes; they were con artists and tricksters. This was the most senior brother, and he initially objected to his sister's marrying a Nigerian, his conclusion being that most Nigerians were the same. Nothing would change his mind or convince him otherwise. In fact, he did not attend our wedding, still holding on to his suspicions. But if you were to ask him now, he would say something different about my marriage to his sister. It has been peaceful, enjoyable, and fruitful, and we have had no reason to invite any of her brothers to settle any form of dispute or problem in our marriage. It has been a success story so far, even when we decided to leave for a mission in another country. According to Sandra's brothers, that would test our marriage. Some said my wife would not go with me to an unknown country or else that she would return after few months. They believed that she would not be able to cope with the lifestyle in Kenya.

Sandra lived with the children and me for five years in Kenya and only returned to attend to her sick brother in 2011. The few months we stayed apart, from February 2011 to May 2011, was the longest absence we had had in our marriage, and we truly missed each other.

Once we had the consent of both our families, we made our intention known to the law, as required by the government, before the wedding would be approved and be allowed to take place. All investigations proved that we had no previous marriages and that neither of us ever had been divorced. I had to present my documents to the authorities for verification. With all documents in order, we could continue with our counselling sessions and whatever preparations we intended to make to marry, both before the law and before the church.

We could then return to our pastor for preparation for premarriage counselling and then to set a wedding date. We had to look at the church calendar before agreeing on a date suitable for the church, and considering our different family schedules, with the expectation that there would be those wanting to travel from Nigeria to attend the wedding in Holland, or those among the family members of my wife-to-be coming from Surinam and other parts of the world.

With our pastor, we agreed that it would be a two-day event. On the first day, we would have the government wedding before the law, and on the second day, we would have the church wedding. So we selected 25 and 26 November 1998 as our wedding dates. With the dates known only to the three of us, the pastor gave us a wedding counsellor from the church: a couple to assist us with the prewedding counselling so the final wedding plans could be made. It was all carefully planned and worked out.

This is an ideal situation, but this is not to say that it works like this in every case. Some churches do not have this type of structure in place, so they rely on the support of church members. Or perhaps you are not a Christian, yet you are reading *Getting to Know You*. If this describes you, know that you still can make use of the experience of people who have gone through successful weddings themselves or who have been part of one.

Provided you have gotten this right—I mean your choice of spouse—it is time to go about planning. Who are those who will help you with your wedding plans? There are now professional bodies called wedding planners, but they will cost you a fortune, whereas if you go through your church, you will spend less and get the right result. I am not in any way against professional wedding planners, but many times they are only interested in the ceremony itself. I am after the preparation of the couple for the wedding.

Getting to Know You will help you and your special friend to work towards that great one-day or two-day occasion in your life. It is a day that will determine the rest of the days of your life. This decision not only will affect the rest of your life but also will determine the course of future generations. It therefore needs more consideration, input, thought, prayer, counsel, and guidance than any other decision you will ever make in your life.

I trust that *Getting to Know You* will help you to make wise decisions and that it will help you to build a good foundation for a lifelong godly and fulfilling marriage.

I once again want to emphasize the principles that you must not ignore or disregard.

Do not be discouraged by differences of opinion or disagreements that may surface during the course of this discussion; that is part of the purpose of *Getting to Know You*. I want you to find out what the two of you may disagree on before your wedding, what problems you may face in the marriage, and what might keep you from a wonderful marriage now or later. The purpose of *Getting to Know You* is not to scare you away from desiring marriage so you come to the conclusion that you won't get married. Many have been scared away from marriage because of the experience of people they know. I was a person who delayed getting married for fear of failure, having witnessed a failed marriage in my own family. I didn't want to repeat the same mistakes or fall into the same cycle of divorce and remarriage. Instead I chose to play it safe by not getting involved. But honestly, that is not a solution on its own. Having children all over the place, keeping a weekend girlfriend, and still coming home to an empty house is not ideal for any man.

Instead it is time to take the bull by the horns. Talk about your differences and fears. Pray about them, get counsel on them, and come to an objective conclusion together on what to do.

It is very difficult to do that once you are married and facing a crisis or a decision that has to be made immediately. The pressure then can cause you to end up fighting, hating and blaming each other for the "wrong decision" you both made at the beginning.

Many times we expect God to fix our mistakes in marriage, but it will take our cooperation and willingness to work on our marriages. God is capable of fixing things for us, but I think that first and foremost, he does not want us to make such a silly mistake by making the wrong choice of life partner and then asking him to fix it. That would be as if you had built your house on sand and then expected God to transfer it to a solid rock. His Word is that we should be wise builders who build on the Rock. So from the start your marriage should be built on rock, not on sand. On the sand, it will be blown away by the winds of life, and the marriage will not stand. I am sorry, but I have to tell you beforehand—and I hope you see it as a warning: build your house on a solid rock, and then God will keep it from the storms and winds of life. Such is the case for marriage too; build it on God, and God will protect it from all the storms of life.

Remember that before you are married, you have not made any covenant yet, so if you find yourself growing increasingly uneasy about getting married right now, or to the person whom you thought was the right person for you, you must share that information with your pastor before the day of the wedding itself. Maybe you need some more time to go back to the drawing board, think it over, and convince yourself that you are ready for marriage. Your pastor can help you step back a bit, develop your relationship with your partner, and address the fears or doubts. Don't be silent on this point. If you are, it could ruin your marriage life forever.

Many times we expect God to fix our mistakes in marriage, but it will take our cooperation and willingness to work on it.

Delay your plans while you both seek God's will together for the relationship.

Never be pressured into marrying. I know of a couple who, after four years of marriage, filed for divorce over reconcilable differences. The woman said she had been cajoled into the marriage by the parents of her husband. They had been very nice to her for years, taking care of her when she needed help the most. Even though she was in love with their son, probably the wedding was too early or too soon after the time they had first started dating. They were not ready for marriage. Even though the wedding was great, after the wedding, the work of the marriage started.

The woman hadn't gotten to know her husband properly before marrying; in the marriage, she said, she felt like a prisoner. That was not nice a word to come out of the mouth of a young wife. The truth was that they didn't get to know each other well enough to accept the lifetime commitment to each other that marriage entails.

For her husband, all he asked for in the early years of their marriage was sex, the result of which is pregnancy. They fought over that because the husband didn't want to be a father yet. So in the four years their marriage lasted, they came out of it with three children. Obviously they had not planned for the children. They had children because they had a regular sex life.

With children came new challenges, which I will discuss in a separate chapter. After three children, the couple was on the verge of a divorce and starting their lives separately again. But now they had three children to cater for in the broken relationship. Before marriage, there is still time to work at the various issues; it is rather delayed than hurrying into a marriage. "Hurry in, hurry out" is not an option.

Prepare yourself adequately for marriage, therefore, to help yourself discover what you need to do. Again, you need the assistance and advice of your pastor, who knows what needs to be done and worked on.

I have carefully researched materials to prepare a marriage checklist of things that need to be taken into consideration and taken care of before you move into the wedding planning stage.

Dr Kevin Omamo Ndai & Carolyne Adienge, now Dr. & Mrs Kevin Omamo Ndai

CHAPTER 8

Who Owns the Marriage?

The first thing that needs to be decided before a couple is even engage is who owns the marriage. I guess to too many people, this is an irrelevant question. The marriage belongs to the man and the woman. I say that is wrong. The marriage does not belong to the man or to the woman. If you have accepted Jesus Christ as Lord and Saviour, then the ownership question is settled: the marriage belongs to God. We have told God that we are totally and completely surrendered to his will; therefore, our wedding plans and the marriage itself shall be under his authority. God wants to bless you and to make you a blessing in the way you handle your marriage. He desires that you and your marriage prosper and that, through your marriage, others come to know him. For marriage is God's institution, and from the very beginning, he ordained for man and woman to come together and live as one.

Marriage should be a union of two people that will last forever. Only in God is such guaranteed.

Under this ownership, we agree to open up our past and to confess all our past and present relationships to God in such a way that he will know there is nothing being hidden before him. Following are some important things to do before marrying:

A. Be prepared for physical openness, for example being willing to obtain an HIV/AIDS test whether we have had past sexual encounters or not. This is to ensure that we are free from any form of sexual disease(s). (This is expected from both the man and the woman.) As you can imagine, since I come from Africa (Nigeria), the first request from my fiancée's family was to see the HIV/AIDS test result before they would let me go further with the relationship. I had already been tested before I met Sandra. The result was negative. I proudly showed my result to her, and she gladly took it to her family, but they rejected it because the test had been done more than a year before I met her. They requested that I do another test, much to her disappointment. Their reason was that I had travelled back to Nigeria since the time of my previous test. Sandra didn't know how to ask me for another test, but I sensed the tension from my conversation with her. I told her I was gladly ready to take another test, and I requested that she accompany me to do the test. She was glad and relieved that I had accepted to do another test. We went to the public health service in Amsterdam (GGD); the doctor, recognizing me, asked why I was doing another test just over a year later. I told him my fiancée's family needed to see the results of a new test. For the first time, in the presence of Sandra, the doctor frightened me when he told me all the implications if my result were positive. Initially I thought, *OK, if the result does not go my way, then there will be no wedding after all,* but I was still convinced that the result would be negative.

After two weeks of an agonizing wait, Sandra and I went together to collect the result. Without opening the envelope, I gave it to her to open, asking her to tell me what the result was. "Negative," she said. Of course that came as a huge relief, but deep down I'd known the result was negative. I didn't demand a similar test from her. She is a nurse, and because of the nature of her job, she had been tested. And she could not lie to me about her status. She was also negative. She underwent regular medical check-ups, including for other diseases I didn't even know of. I trusted that she would have informed me if there had been anything I needed to know before we started talking about wedding. In our openness to one another, we talked sincerely. I requested that from her.

With our medicals clear, we had fewer hurdles in our way, so we could continue talking about and preparing for a wedding.

People struggle with this type of openness. I know of two persons who communicate better through email and text messages than they do in face-to-face communication. I told them that their situation was none too pleasant. "Don't hide behind the media apparatus. What happens after your wedding? Will you be communicating with your wife through emails and text messages?" I discovered that one of these people was not being truthful in the relationship, so the couple were not going anywhere yet.

B. Confess any sexual sin (relationships) you have committed before now or any sexual addictions, such as to pornography or masturbation, so that you can be freed from them. Listen, this is the build-up to a lifetime relationship. Any hidden secret will come out into the light inside the marriage, and it will damage the marriage. It could even destroy the marriage.

I know of a couple who no longer have sexual intercourse after three children, yet the husband wakes up in the middle of the night to watch pornography on his computer. He no longer finds his wife attractive enough to have sexual intercourse with; he rather lives in his fantasies. This is wrong. If you are in a similar situation, then I encourage you to talk about the problem and seek for a solution to it. In the marriage I'm talking about here, the wife was aware that her husband watched pornography and had no sexual interest in her, but she did not know how to address the problem. Before you knew it, the wife, too, was going outside the marriage, seeking sexual attention and satisfaction elsewhere. This is a problem from the past that had not been dealt with, and it came to hurt the marriage. There is still a way out of this situation if both of them will be honest enough to admit their past problems and deal with them. I recommend spiritual counselling in a situation such as this one. Divorce is not a solution, but helping the couple to work through the challenges and make their marriage attractive again to each other is.

I give tips to married couples on how to make themselves attractive again to each other, particularly the woman. When a wife wears jeans or trousers to bed, what can she expect from her husband? I give more tips to people when they are married. Just know that there are no restrictions on how you should enjoy yourself. Your husband is yours, and you are his.

I will discuss more on this aspect of marriage in a later chapter. It is one of the areas in which marriages these days are struggling, namely lack of sexual satisfaction from one partner or the other.

C. Open yourself up to the hurtful memories of a past relationship which has caused bitterness and unforgiveness.

You need a trusted counsellor to discuss these matters with. You must note that asking forgiveness for sexual immorality is a form of protection against its happening again to you. You have exposed it to the light; therefore, the guilt no longer ties you to the sin. For instance, a female who had been raped would probably be scared in an open relationship leading to marriage and afraid to talk about it. It may also be a difficult subject to discuss with her partner. Therefore, she needs a good counsellor to disclose this information to, and she needs to talk about it with her partner. She needs to deal with it and be helped through it. An easier way would be if she had a supportive husband by her side who would not call her names or use such hurtful memories to terrorize her when the two of them had misunderstandings in the relationship. There are negative other experiences that can affect a marriage partner, such as abusive parents, incest in the family, sexual harassment at school or even from family members, and a previously abusive relationship with someone of the opposite sex. Whatever the situation may be, please find someone to talk with about it, preferably a professional counsellor and a godly person. Once you deal with this painful memory, you will enjoy your new relationship in Christ and your marriage.

Avoid generalizations, saying that all men—or all women—are the same. See your new relationship as it is, as a new relationship with a new person.

D. Be determined to stay pure and devoted to Jesus Christ and to your marriage.

From here until death do you part, you have been given the visa to cross into the realm of marriage and enter into the fraternity. Like I said earlier, once you get to this stage of talking about marrying, you renounce every other form of friendship and any old need to seize, and you totally give yourself to your new lifetime project. Marriage is not a celebrity show where you watch for how many controversies you can create. Both partners must be determined to keep the relationship pure.

A brother who was preparing for marriage admitted to having cheated on his fiancée a few months before their wedding. What a shame! It took the intervention of the Holy Spirit to save the relationship. It was an old girlfriend who had come to give him a "parting gift", which was sex. The woman was just evil, wanting to put asunder what God was putting together.

The brother came clean of the sin to his partner. Although the wedding was postponed and they began to work on their relationship again, they finally got married and lived happily thereafter. Now they are blessed with children.

Marriage is not a celebrity show where you watch for how many controversies you can create.

My beloved evangelist, Chuck Turner of Victory Outreach International, in one of his teachings said that dating is false advertising. I asked him to explain. He said that many mistake marriage as a continuation of dating, rather than realizing that marriage needs to be guided by the values of dating, where you showed so much respect and reverence to your girlfriend. Do you remember the days when you opened the car door for her first? Do you remember when you brought those beautiful flowers to express how much you loved her? How about when you ordered breakfast to be brought to her at home first thing in the morning! I could go on and on. So, what happens after the wedding? Bring back that dating experience to your marriage, and you will begin to enjoy your marriage.

Our marriage has been so peaceful, enjoyable, and fruitful, and we have had no reason to invite anyone to settle any form of dispute or problem in our marriage.

CHAPTER 9

Spiritual Oneness

It is not enough merely to seek a life partner with whom to live in the same house. The idea of living together and turning it into marriage is not proper. Genesis 1:26–27 gives us the foundation of who we are meant to be when we come together in marriage. "Then God said, let us make man in our image, according to our likeness; so God created man in His own image; the image of God He create him; male and female He created them." This scripture also explains God's intention in that he created two sexes—male and female—in his likeness, but he never intended people of the same sex to be joined in his likeness. The two, male and female, are to become inseparable in him.

If the husband and wife were made in the image of God, who is not separated, then we can learn about our relationship as husband and wife from the God of relationships with his Son and his Holy Spirit, all three of whom, we believe, are one. Read the following scriptures and see for yourself the relationship between God the Father, God the Son, and God the Holy Spirit:

- "And all Mine are Yours, and Yours are mine, and I am glorified in them" (John 17:10).
- "That they all may be one, as You, Father, are in Me, and I in you, that thy also may be one in us, that the world may believe that you sent Me" (John 17:21).
- Jesus said, "If you had known Me, you would have known My Father also" (John 14:7).

Based on these statements, I truly believe that God wants a union of two people (male and female) who will become one, doing things in oneness, togetherness, and unity of mind and purpose. Therefore, spiritual oneness is the essential key to marriage. I am not surprised that many marriages are not binding; this is because there is no spiritual oneness in the union. A man who has four women has no spiritual oneness, at least not in God's view.

Now it would be interesting if we could apply these statements to the husband wife relationship. Look at the marriage traditions around you. Do they comply with God's original intention? I ask you to consider these questions and give your answers to assess your relationship and see if it is in line with God's wishes:

a. Do you agree and accept that the husband is the head of the household?

b. Do you agree and accept that the wife serves the purposes of the husband?

c. Do you agree and accept that husband and wife know each other so well that the wife knows what to do without even being told?

d. Do you agree and accept that the husband and the wife do the planning together in the marriage?

e. Do you agree and accept that the wife does what she thinks is best and only consults with her husband when it is absolutely necessary?

f. Do you agree and accept that husband and wife sit together and plan, and that the children can be assured that decisions are made by both of them together for their common interest?

g. Do you agree and accept that the husband and wife have divided and divine responsibilities according to their strengths and abilities in the marriage?

h. Do you agree and accept that the wife is not less important than the husband?

I imagine that the womenfolk are probably shaking their heads in total disagreement with me, but my purpose here is not to cause any confusion. My purpose is to ask you to compare notes and reason together. Marriage is a union of communication. See what you disagree on; make notes and observations about the union; and talk it over together. You may not totally agree with me, but I have given you food for thought with regards to how you can work on your marriage and make it even better than I have suggested. If you have yet to marry but you are working towards it, compare notes with your friend and see what he or she thinks about the opinions I have expressed above. Let your answers be based on biblical principles only and not on emotional feelings or sentiments, or on what someone else says is workable for him or her.

The answers you arrive at should help to make clear the traditional views of a man and a woman in a relationship. How do you understand the traditional perspective on the husband–wife relationship, namely that the wife should be seen but not heard, with only an assigned role to play?

What does the scripture teach us in Genesis 2:18–25?

And the Lord God said, "It is not good that man should be alone; I will make him a helper comparable to him."

And the Lord God caused a deep sleep to fall on Adam, and he slept; and He took one of his ribs and closed up the flesh in its place. Then the rib, which the Lord God has taken from the man, He made into a woman, and He brought her to the man. And Adam said: "This is now bone of my bones and flesh of my flesh. She shall be called Woman, because she was taken out of Man." And they were both naked, the man and his wife, and were not ashamed.

You may say that these scriptures were written in the old days, before Adam sinned and changed the dynamics of God's plan, but the principle and value of marriage was established with these two persons who were created first.

"Sin came into the world through one man, and his sin brought death with it. As a result, death has spread to the whole human race because everyone has sinned." Romans 5:12 explains that first sin and how it brought sin to the whole world.

So in the space following, let us look at New Testament scriptures that might help us to understand the roles of husband and wife even better.

Marriage—Christ and the Church

At no time did God diminish the institution of marriage he established with the first man, Adam, and the first woman, Eve.

Roles for Wives

Submitting to one another in the fear of God

"Wives, submit to your own husbands, as to the Lord. For the husband is head of the wife, as also Christ is head of the church; and He is the Savior of the body. Therefore, just as the church is subject to Christ, so let the wives be to their own husbands in everything" (Ephesians 5:21–33).

In this New Testament scripture we find a clear role defined for women (wives). It is crystal clear what is expected of wives, but also the role of men in marriage is very clear. The simple act of obedience to the Word of God makes marriage simple and workable. Submission does not mean inequality, as some have translated it to be, but mutual respect and regard for one another.

Roles for Husbands

> Husbands, love your wives, just as Christ also loved the church and gave Himself for her, that He might sanctify and cleanse her with the washing of water by the word, that He might present her to Himself a glorious church, not having spot or wrinkle or any such thing, but that she should be holy and without blemish. So husbands ought to love their own wives as their own bodies; he who loves his wife loves himself. For no one ever hated his own flesh, but nourishes and cherishes it, just as the Lord does the church. For we are members of His body, of His flesh and of His bones. "For this reason a man shall leave his father and mother and be joined to his wife and the two shall become one flesh." This is a great mystery, but I speak concerning Christ and the church. Nevertheless let each one of you in particular so love his own wife as himself, and let the wife see that she respects her husband. (Ephesians 25–33)

In Colossians 3:18–19, we see a shorter version of the role of wives and husbands, expressed in a very straightforward statement: "Wives, submit to your own husbands, as is fitting in the Lord. Husbands, love your wives and do not be bitter toward them."

In 1 Peter 3:1–9, we read from the Word of God that it is a specific instruction for wives to obey their husbands in order to maintain harmony in their marriage.

Listen, it is not a conditional request. As I hear some people say, "You don't know my wife [or husband]. She [or he] is not lovable." If such is the case, then why did they marry that person?

Breaking down these scriptures, I believe what they are saying is simply that husbands are the heads of the marriage not only by mouth but also by responsibility. A man should make his wife to be the best. Whatever you are going to desire in another woman should be present in your wife, and if it is not there, provide it for her. Beauty is in the eye of the beholder, the familiar adage says, so make your wife beautiful. Meet her basic needs in the marriage and see if your wife will not submit to your authority.

I often hear some men tell their wives, "I am your husband." The wife knows that the only difference is that her husband is not acting as husband but merely stating the fact that he is her husband. Begin to act as a husband, and she will treat you as such. Simple!

Submission to Husbands

> Wives, likewise, be submissive to your own husbands, that even if some do not obey the word, they, without a word, may be won by the conduct of their wives, when they observe your chaste conduct accompanied by fear. Do not let your adornment be merely outward—arranging the hair, wearing gold, or putting on fine apparel—rather, let it be the hidden person of the heart, with the incorruptible beauty of a gentle and quiet spirit, which is very precious in the sight of God. For in this manner, in former times, the holy women who trusted in God also adorned themselves, being submissive to their own husbands, as Sarah obeyed Abraham, calling him Lord, whose daughters you are if you do good and are not afraid with any terror. (1 Peter 3:1–6)

For young women, either married or not, this is a perfect virtue you can imitate from the Bible. Consider the humility of Sarah as recorded in the Bible. Her respect for her husband came from the inside—in her spirit—and only manifested on the outside.

For some women of today, we have to teach them everything from the outside in because they don't have these things inside them. They keep forgetting how to treat their husbands nicely.

A Word for Husbands

"Husbands, likewise, dwell with them with understanding, giving honour to the wife, as to the weaker vessel, and as being heirs together of the grace of life, that your prayers may not be hindered" (1 Peter 3:7).

A man who does not treat his wife well or properly is denying himself his blessings and progress in life. So, if you have been wondering why you are not progressing, it might not be witchcraft or other vices. Check your home front. How are you treating your wife at home? Honour her, make her the crown of your head. If she is a thorn, then I imagine you will constantly have a headache. Make her the crown; then you can have peace.

> A man should make his wife to be the best. Whatever you are going to desire in another woman is in your wife. And if it is not there, provide it for her.

Called to Blessing

"All of you be of one mind, having compassion for one another; love as brothers, be tender hearted, be courteous; not returning evil for evil or reviling for reviling, but on the contrary, bless, knowing that you were called to this, that you may inherit a blessing" (1 Peter 3:8–9).

The man and woman should bless one another. Even before you get married, begin to pray for each other and pour out blessings upon each other. A husband's blessing is for the wife, and a wife's blessing is for the husband. You are one.

I remember some arguments that came up during a counselling session. A woman asked me if it was not proper that men should consider that women are the weaker partner or weaker vessel as recorded in 1 Peter 3:7. I totally agree with the scripture. The scripture is clear when it describes the woman as the weaker sex, but it also causes us to realize that she is a joint heir—an equal not in size but in terms of benefiting in the marriage. She is an equal partner, not a lesser being in the marriage. Also, there is actually a medical explanation that confirms that women are weaker vessels, as mentioned in the Bible. You could ask your personal doctor about this assertion.

According to medical examiners, a woman's blood contains more water and 20 per cent fewer red blood cells. Since the red blood cells supply oxygen to the body, women tire more quickly than men. There might even be a bigger problem if the blood that the woman loses each month causes her to become anaemic (not enough iron to build the red blood cells). On the other hand, men generally possess 50 per cent more strength than women, and 40 per cent of a man's body weight is muscle, compared to 23 per cent of a woman's.

And women deal with various hormonal issues throughout the month that can cause physical problems and emotional weakness as well. Therefore, for these reasons, men need to deal with women with *understanding*. In fact, men should dwell in understanding for a woman. The Word of God is true. If we pay attention to it, it guarantees all solutions to all problematic situations. Why?

The woman, despite the weakness that I have pointed out, is a woman of virtue. Read Proverbs 31:10–31:

The Virtuous Wife

Who can find a virtuous wife?
For her worth is far above rubies.
The heart of her husband safely trusts her
So he will have no lack of gain.
She does him good and not evil
All the days of her life.
She seeks wool and flax,
And willingly works with her hands.
She is like the merchant ships,
She brings her food from afar.
She also rises while it is yet night,
And provides food for her household,

And a portion for her maidservants.
She considers a field and buys it;
From her profits she plants a vineyard.
She girds herself with strength,
And strengthens her arms.
She perceives that her merchandise is good,
And her lamp does not go out by night.
She stretches out her hands to the distaff,
And her hand holds the spindle.
She extends her hand to the poor,
Yes, she reaches out her hands to the needy.
She is not afraid of snow for her household,
For all her household is clothed with scarlet.
She makes tapestry for herself;
Her clothing is fine linen and purple.
Her husband is known in the gates,
When he sits among the elders of the land.
She makes linen garments and sells them,
And supplies sashes for the merchants.
Strength and honor are her clothing;
She shall rejoice in time to come.
She opens her mouth with wisdom,
And on her tongue is the law of kindness.
She watches over the ways of her household,
And does not eat the bread of idleness.
Her children rise up and call her blessed;
Her husband also, and he praises her:
"Many daughters have done well,
But you excel them all."
Charm is deceitful and beauty is passing,
But a woman who fears the Lord, she shall be praised.
Give her of the fruit of her hands,
And let her own works praise her in the gates.

Consider also, "But if anyone does not provide for his own, and especially for those of his household, he has denied the faith and is worse than an unbeliever" (1 Timothy 5:8).

The question that introduces a woman in Proverbs 31:10 blows my mind. If only women knew what they were made of, the substance that is in them, they probably would carry themselves much better than they do now.

Woman, you are not second class or weaker in that sense, but are a strong helper for your husband. Actually, the woman helps bring a balance to the marriage, particularly the home and family, including the man.

"Who can find a virtuous wife? For her worth is far above rubies." Another translation phrases it as "A woman of noble character who can find?"

Responsibilities

"Then God blessed them, and God said to them, 'Be fruitful and multiply; fill the earth and subdue it; have dominion (rule) over the fish of the sea, over the birds of the air, and over every living thing that moves on the earth'" (Genesis 1:22).

This is another responsibility that can be fulfilled only by a man and woman joined in union as approved by God and not otherwise. The issue today is that many are becoming fruitful without following the principle laid down by God—that behaviours are acts arising from not listening to God's Word or what we call disobedience towards God. You don't need any person to point a finger at you, for you to know that what you are doing is wrong. I advise you to stop it and turn towards the path of truth and righteousness.

It is very clear from the beginning what God intended in the relationship between a man and a woman when they come together in marriage. It is a five-point responsibility that you can find in the scripture which reads, "Then God blessed them, and God said to them, 'Be fruitful and multiply; fill the earth and subdue it; have dominion (rule) over the fish of the sea, over the birds of the air, and over every living thing that moves on the earth.'"

1. Be fruitful.
2. Multiply.
3. Fill.
4. Subdue.
5. Have dominion (rule).

None of this is complete without the other facets in the true sense of God's perfect intention. God does not intend us to separate them; we should take them together in their completion.

If you study the Bible carefully, you will find various responsibilities given to humankind by God. In Ephesians and 1 Peter, and also in 1 Timothy 5:8, we see additional responsibilities given to man and woman. I would call out some more of these, but you need to discover more and discuss scripture among yourselves as part of your preparation for marriage.

In similar circumstances, men are given certain responsibilities, and women are given certain responsibilities. Read Proverbs 31:10–31. For the sake of my argument, I will point out some of the responsibilities of the woman (wife). I don't think these guidelines are meant only for these particular situations but are meant for every woman who aspires to become a wife someday. She should be willing to do these things to please her husband. This aspect of her responsibilities does not make a woman a slave to the man or a lesser being than the man. The responsibilities are:

a. Shopping for food
b. Administering the household
c. Buying land and developing it

  d. Doing volunteer work
  e. Providing clothes for the family
  f. Decorating the home
  g. Having her own small or large business

Two verses in chapter 31 of Proverbs tell us how the husband of this woman responds. In verse 11, we read, "The heart of her husband trusts in her and he will have no lack of gain." Verse 28 reads, "Her children rise up and call her blessed, her husband also, and he praises her." I guess every wife wants a husband who praises her. If this describes you, then take responsibility and do the things I have suggested above. You will be the apple of his eye alone.

From the points I have listed here, it is obvious that each person is given responsibilities in the marriage. You need to know of these responsibilities before you enter into a marriage. Secondly, you need to help one another to develop the gifts and abilities given by God to achieve a successful marriage.

You may not totally agree with me, but I have given you food for thought on how you can work on your marriage and make it even better than I have suggested.

It must be noted that it is not a competition to discover who is better or best or who is weaker in the marriage. Rather, the purpose is to look and to see each other as a companion to the other person rather than a helper of the weaker person. People often ask me if I don't have issues with my wife. Yes I do, but I just don't allow the bins to spill out of my house or go out of control. We deal with our issues as two mature people who understand what marriage is all about. Up till now, we have never invited a third party to mediate in our marriage. First we take any problems to God in prayer; then we talk about it again and again until we resolve the difference.

During your dating period, it would be great if you would make a checklist of what you are good at and the things your partner is good at also. Then compare notes. And be honest about your list because it will determine how the other person relates to you in that particular area.

I will place in a chart some assumptions for you, and I expect you to honestly tick what you think of the statement in terms of your relationship with your partner.

	1—Agree	2—Disagree	3—Not sure
The husband is the head of the household.			
The husband's first responsibility is to himself.			
The husband's first responsibility is to his job.			
The wife should not take up employment outside her home responsibilities.			

The wife's only responsibility is to keep the home neat and clean.			
The wife should always be the one to cook.			
The money the husband earns is his money.			
The money the wife earns is her money.			
Children develop better in a home where parents are strict disciplinarians.			
The husband should take the wife out somewhere special once a month,			
The husband should seek the counsel of his wife on all decisions affecting the family.			

1. Do this exercise separately, but compare your answers together.
2. Discuss the subjects you disagree on.
3. Try to rewrite those areas you disagree on in such a way that both of you can agree. For instance, if you do not agree that only the woman should cook, then you rewrite it to read, "Both husband and wife shall share the responsibility of cooking in the home."

From the beginning, I have had an understanding with my wife that I would help her in the kitchen. The kitchen is not the sole responsibility of my wife. Listen, she is not entirely a housewife; she works to support the whole family, so why shouldn't I help her in the kitchen? Without having to rely on a roster, I cook when she is not there or when she is tired and wanting my help at home. Interestingly, my wife enjoys my cooking, as do the kids. And it is not because I am a better cook but because Daddy cooked.

Interestingly, my wife enjoys my cooking, as do the kids. It is not because I am a better cook but because Daddy cooked.

Elvis & Sandra on our wedding day over 22 years ago
Now Pastor & Mrs. Elvis Iruh

CHAPTER 10

Financial Oneness

This is probably the most controversial subject when it comes to wedding planning. In fact, many couple wouldn't want to talk about it, especially since it is the centre of everything that would happen in putting the wedding together? Now, just to forewarn you, this chapter is not about spending in the marriage or what your financial status is.

What is your financial standing before your wedding and going into a marriage? You need to know what both of you have, comparing this to what you are planning to do. God shall not provide without careful planning on your end. Both of you need to address your financial state before the wedding. What is each one of you bringing along into the marriage? I am not talking about professing love. There can be no amount of love that helps one achieve financial stability, without which the marriage will be tested, probably rocking the boat even before it starts sailing. Let there be financial consideration before and after the wedding, centred on the issues which follow:

A. An understanding of your financial situation will help decide your budgeting for the wedding. I would warn you—and I'll explain later—do not depend on others for money when you're planning your wedding. Of course, you may accept support when it comes, but if you depend on other people to finance your wedding, what will happen when they disappoint you? Several couples I know have experienced relying on others for the money they promised, only for the money not to arrive, at which point the couples needed to turn to plan B. Make a solid arrangement with regards to your resources at the beginning. Then, whatever else comes in as assistance is a bonus.

B. Discuss any debts you have at the very beginning, knowing that you may have to combine your finances once you are married. Leave nothing out. Resist the urge to say that it is not important for now. You must make a plan to implement a debt-free approach as quickly as possible, and you must let your partner know what the situation is from the beginning. Nobody wants to pay the other person's debt, particularly when they didn't know anything about it. If your partner already knows and decides to help out, praise God and accept his or her help.

C. Make a financial commitment to God. What about your financial commitment to God (tithing) in the first instance? Do you suspend your tithe in favour of your wedding plans? Or reduce your tithe until after you are married? Your tithe is nonnegotiable and should not be touched in any way, neither during your dating period nor after your wedding. Both of you have to tithe separately until you are married, at which time you can begin to tithe together as one family. This does not include personal blessings that you want to tithe to the Lord. Your tithe needs to be personal with God until you and your spouse-to-be become one. If you have separate salaries, you need to tithe on your salaries separately, but once you are blessed as husband and wife, you should do it together.

When you finally get married, don't use your family budget (money for the house, food, and so forth) to pay your tithe. Make sure that the tithe is first agreed to and then taken out before any other consideration because it is money set aside for God. This is the honourable and respectful thing to do.

D. How are your saving habits? Do you have separate savings before your wedding? Do you plan to have one savings account when you eventually get married? You must begin to think of financial oneness with your partner where you do not hide anything from him or her when it comes to financial matters. I know different cultures have different ideas about finances in marriage. According to some cultures, women should not know how money is brought in to, or spent by, the family. In some cultures, the woman is the bank of the family and keeps all the money. Whatever method you choose to follow, let it be transparent to both of you.

E. Commit yourself in your heart to hold all the money in common. It is important that your money soon becomes "our money" when you are married. Let money be safe with both of you, and use your money wisely for the honour and glory of God and your new family. Doing things together to achieve financial accountability as a family is recommended from the start.

**No amount of love can prevent financial stability, which would probably test the marriage and rock the boat.
Let there be financial consideration before and after marriage.**

CHAPTER 11

Ministerial Oneness

Understanding where both of you are in Christ Jesus before you accept to marry each other is very important. Have you accepted Christ as your Saviour? Do you belong to a church? Were you involved in ministry prior to meeting your partner? How do you see your future in ministry after your wedding? Do you intend to move forward together in the ministry of God's church after your wedding? These are possible scenarios you must talk about and agree to work together on. As Christians, you would likely find it enjoyable to work together in ministry, although it is not compulsory that both of you be in ministry. If you were not called into ministry, just being a good Christian is a starting point.

Being faithful in ministry will demand much from you, and it is probably making demands right now on your relationship. It demands your time, doing a good job for the Lord. I must say, listening; taking instructions and obeying them; being honest about your responsibilities; and being a man or a woman of integrity are all abilities you develop by being faithful in ministry.

How does your partner see your involvement with ministry? Does he or she think it is too demanding, or is he or she pleased for you and even expecting you to do more for God? Is your partner willing to work with you or give you the necessary support that would be of help to your marriage by bringing understanding to what you do for God? Even if you intend to be an ordinary Christian without any form of direct commitment to ministry, you need to be together on this. "A family that prays together, stays together" is a popular adage. I still think you stand to benefit more by being involved in ministry together than by being a bystander or onlooker. Encourage one another to be involved in church ministry; it is healthy and brings about a better understanding in the union. I cannot imagine, if my wife were not involved in ministry with me from the beginning, how it would have been when I received my calling as a pastor and decided to work for God, even going abroad to another nation to do the work of ministry.

Sandra automatically became a pastor's wife, and that came with its own responsibilities and, of course, challenges. Even if it meant only that she had to stand with me and support me to fulfil the call of God upon my life, that was challenging enough. From the very beginning, I encouraged her to be part of the ministry. She does not see herself as a preacher, but she is a preacher's wife and she helps with Sunday school, working with the children. She does office administration and heads the women ministry. This is enough work in the ministry.

The experience helped her in the future endeavours we undertook together with me as a pastor. It would have been difficult for her to just one day decide to go with me on mission to a foreign country without the experience of working together in the ministry. What would she be doing? Since we have lived our lives together as Christians involved in ministry, she understood the calling upon my life and the demands. She adequately coped with it throughout our five years abroad.

Consider taking care of anything from your past that may hurt your ministry, in case someone wants to accuse you now or in the future about your conduct prior to now. There are people out there who are mischievous in their objectives. Do you know that? Has your husband-to-be told you that he used to use drugs or that he was a drunkard or a womanizer? Has he yet told you that he used to be a thief or that he has a dark past? Yes, he did? He is clean now, and the past is past. What would your reaction be if, for instance, you caught him stealing or cheating on you with one of his past partners? How would you handle these matters? Let me tell you the honest truth: if your spouse-to-be has the boldness to admit his or her past mistakes, then you should help him or her to walk through it and not use it to hurt him or her again.

The best friend anyone can have is one who tells you the truth—the whole truth. We encourage that in the ministry so that a person's past does not become a stumbling block on the way to his or her future.

Encourage one another to be involved in church ministry. It is healthy and brings about a better understanding in the union.

CHAPTER 12

Tying Down a Relationship

For five years, I worked as a missionary pastor based in Kisumu, Kenya. During those years, I travelled around the country ministering the gospel. On several occasions, women approached me for counselling, and most of their questions were about their inability to tie down a relationship with a man so it would eventually lead to marriage. These women all spoke of a relationship of several years, yet the question of marriage never arose. Once the subject of marriage appeared on the menu card, all the men walked away or developed cold feet and gradually disengaged from the relationship. Within months, the relationships were over. Some men may outright tell you they are not ready for marriage yet.

In my attempt to find out the cause of this problem, I spoke to a couple of women, but I didn't get much from them. The story was that the man was not ready yet, and the women were worried that they were ageing fast. Some had actually been in a stable relationship with plans to get married, but before the couple could agree on the wedding plans, the relationship suddenly ended. One woman in particular disclosed to me how she had waited seven years for a man who promised to marry her. The relationship had started back in Kenya, then the guy left for the United States of America. They continued to communicate, and the promise of marriage was still in the cards. She was very hopeful; she was kept tied down by the sporadic gifts he sent to her from United States. In the first few weeks of his travels, he called nearly every other day, but as the months passed by, the phone calls decreased in number. Now she only speaks to his answering machine on the other end, and he rarely bothers to return her calls. When he does return her call, he speaks only a few words—claiming to be busy as usual.

When she asks about their relationship, he simply jokes about it and tells her to wait; he will soon be back in Kenya to make wedding plans. So she has been waiting for seven years. I asked her if they had been involved in any form of counselling before he left for abroad. Her reply was "No."

In fact, he is not a Christian, whereas she is a devoted Christian and prayerful in all her doings. She had hoped that he would change with time, and of course her emotions, in time, developed into a supposed relationship with the promise of marriage as part of the bargain. I advised her to forget about the relationship, as it never existed in the first place. The relationship simply was based on emotions and feelings. "I love him and he loved me," she declared. I told her, "I see no sign of love in your story. If he loves you, he will commit himself to the relationship." The basic approach to a good relationship, namely communication, was not there. It had evaporated into thin air—vanished.

Lack of communication from the onset of the relationship was a key factor in the failure of the relationship. She never really got to know the man; the relationship was based on her excitement of a dream for their future together. Dreams you never work on will never come to pass; believe me. It remains just a dream. Despite my advice to this young woman, she continued to live in denial, dreaming that the guy was still planning to come for her one day.

During the Christmas season of 2008, she travelled to her rural home to visit her family, and to her surprise she met her long-awaited man in their home town. He had not come for her as he'd promised, but he'd come home with another woman he had married in the United States—to officially introduce her to his Kenyan parents. They'd already had the civil wedding in the United States and were blessed with a child. Unfortunately, Sister Ann, as I choose to call her, even knew the woman this man was now married to. In fact, the women had been college schoolmates before Ann travelled abroad after her education. They happened to know each other, and they happened to have come from the same village. So while this man kept Ann waiting on the other side of the world, in Kenya, he already had found another love, and he was planning on moving on with his life without having the courage to inform Ann of his decision so she could also move on with her life. Yes, his actions were wicked and ungodly. I find such behaviour highly irresponsible. Many people still act in this way. Be sure of what you are getting into before committing your life to a dream.

Of course Sister Ann couldn't believe her eyes; she was heartbroken, bitter, and disillusioned about men and relationships. The next question she asked was "How could I have known he was deceiving me?" It is not difficult to see when a relationship is not what it should be. The signs were there, but she chose not to believe them or act on them, preferring to hold on to illusions. Thank God she is picking up the pieces of her life and moving on. I hope that she has learnt a lesson from this experience, as bitter as it might have been.

One day I jokingly asked a carpenter friend of mine in Kisumu, a young, handsome, hardworking man, when he planned to get marry. He replied, "Pastor, you don't know Kenyan women, particularly Luo women. They don't love you; they are only after your money. They are not interested in marriage. I can't find a good woman." I asked him if he knew what the Luo women were saying about the Luo men—the same things the men were saying about the women: that they're no good, they're lazy, they're only looking for a rich woman, or else a woman with a job, to marry. Obviously, lack of understanding and lack of effective communication gives room for misinformation and poor judgement of people. There is nothing wrong with Luo men or women; they are basing their ideas on generalizations. I have seen some Luo men in good marriages. My good friend Bishop Dr George Kennedy is married to my Nigerian sister Elizabeth Kennedy, also a pastor, and their marriage is a good example. We all worked together on marital issues in our churches.

Angela (not her real name) is a beautiful twenty-six-year-old Luo woman, one of the last young women I met before I left Kisumu to return to Europe after completing my mission work. She is a nurse who came to visit our church a couple of times, and she and I got to talking. During my discussion with her, I asked her about her personal life and if she was involved in a relationship. She told me, "No."

I asked, "Why?"

She is a career person, so I sensed that attitude of independence in her, along the lines of *I don't need a man.* "Not yet. And if I do decide to get married, then I have to move away from here. I will never marry a Luo man. They are not romantic; they are lazy, dirty, wicked, and abusive."

"Have you ever had relationship with a Luo man?" I asked.

She replied, "No." She had friends who had had bad experiences with Luo men. For her this was enough of a warning sign. Then she shocked me by pleading with me for assistance. "Please, Pastor, if you find a nice white man in your country looking for a wife from Kenya, kindly remember me." I couldn't believe what I'd heard from her. She thought a white man was better than a Luo man. She thought marrying a white man was a solution to her martial predicament in Kenya. I know she was probably not the only person thinking this way. From experience, I know that many Kenyan women flock round white men at the beach with this hope of finding a white man to marry them. All that glitters is not gold, meaning that a white man may not be a better husband than a Kenyan man. I totally disagree that white men are better than Kenyan men, and I have enough information to write a book on the subject.

I continued to tease Angela, hoping to find out why she would rather choose a white man as a husband. "White men are more romantic," she said!

"Have you ever dated one before?"

"No," she replied.

"So how do you know white men are more romantic?"

My guess was that she got the idea from watching too much television. Kenyan television is filled with all these soap operas from South America with all sorts of love stories. Stop kidding me! This type of generalization is dangerous in that it exposes women, particularly African women, to unnecessary danger, exploitation, and the possibility of being trapped for life. I could tell you several stories of terrible relationships between white men and black women, particularly Africans, some of them badly brutalized, but again, it has nothing to do with being white or black. In Europe, I also hear stories of African women who married white men because they thought they were better than black men. Love has no colour, at least from my understanding; love is for all people of every colour or race. Again, I think Angela got this idea from watching too many Western movies, a lot of them on Kenyan television—romance dramas. That type of dramatized-for-television love does not exist in real life. You have to have a real love experience, not watch all that trash on television.

Angela asked me alternatively for a Nigerian man. That sentiment was one that came from Nigerian home videos (Nollywood). Nollywood's television stations are filled with Nigerian home videos showing that all the nice-looking Nigerian men are not married and that they have a lot of money to spend. Angela asked me why those rich Nigerian men weren't married and if they should come to Kenya to find beautiful brides. Movies are make-believe. Most of the stories they tell are not true; they're the product of someone's imagination. Marriage is not about being good-looking or having a fat bank account, a good salary, or any other material thing. Although such items contribute to a successful marriage, they do not guarantee a good marriage and are not the primary goal of marriage. The primary goal is a relationship based on God's Word and purpose, trusting in him, planning with him in mind, and executing those plans in his grace.

All that glitters is not gold. A white man may not be a better husband than a Kenyan man.

I have personally witnessed tremendous stress in many mixed marriages, that is in a marriage between a white person and a black person. The success of the marriage has nothing to do with the colour of the spouses. If the two have a good understanding of each other and sincerely love each other, colour should not be an issue. I have seen interracial marriages stand the test of time, lasting over five decades, until death do them part. The list of people I have encountered with successful stories is longer than the list of failures, but the success is not based on wishes. It is based on two people who sincerely work hard on their marriage.

In the various places I visited during my stay in Kenya, I was confronted with issues related to marriage. The number of times I was asked to speak on relationships is hard to count. I picked some stories about these people to share with you in *Getting to Know You* because I believe that the story of one person probably represents the story of thousands of others going through the same situation.

Another woman sent me this email: "Pastor, I am fine but a bit frustrated. My siblings are on my back. They want me to get married despite my having told them that I am not ready yet. They call me every day to remind me of the same thing. What can I do?" I know that in Africa, most young women are under this type of pressure from their families, who seem not to care if these women are sincerely ready for marriage or if they end up with a happy relationship based on true love that might lead to marriage. Some families arrange marriages for their daughters and organize the wedding, forcing them to marry, but often the experience turns out not to be in the best interests of the family. Then there are the women who are just trying to please their parents and other family members, or they're wanting to be like their friends who are either married or in a living-together relationship.

Don't be pressured into a relationship to please your parents, your siblings, your friends, or anyone else. If you are not the main consideration in the relationship, then stop it. You will get hurt in it. Again, I repeat, marriage is for you and nobody else. Those same family members will reject you when your husband throws you out of his house. They'll ask you, "Did we force that man on you?" My advice is simple: don't rush into marriage, or else you will rush out of it.

Another woman in Nakuru, Kenya, wrote this to me after ministering in their church: "I am supposed to be married by now—I am in my thirties—but what do I get? Heartbreak. I am depressed, disappointed, frustrated—you name it. Every day I ask myself why I was born into this world. I have not yet seen a man who loves me for who I am. I chase men away because what they come after is sex before marriage, and I won't give my body to any man except the man who will ultimately become my husband. But up till now I haven't been able to find the right man."

First things first: age should not be a concern. You are not too old at thirty-plus to be married. People are getting married at a much older age now. The important thing is to marry the right man ordained for you by God, and then you will enjoy your marriage. Just wait upon the Lord and keep yourself pure as you have done up till now. Engage yourself in seeking the face of God instead of being frustrated. The Lord will bring you the right man at the right time, and you will see it. My wife was in her midthirties when we met, and finally we got married. We are blessed with children in the marriage.

I met Grace (not her real name) in Kampala, Uganda. She is a graduate of Makerere University. She was not in a relationship at the time of our discussion. She is a woman with strong will, very determined to remain a virgin until the right man comes her way. Few men had approached her in the past, but once she made known her position, they vanished because they wanted sex before marriage. I totally agree with her resolve, her strong point, and her view on sex as a condition of a relationship or even a marriage. I totally support and agree with her view that giving yourself away and having sex is not a guarantee that the man you have sex with will marry you. I minister to young women who are in a love relationship, advising them not to give in to sexual pressure as a condition of the relationship or of marriage. I counsel them to internalize the idea *If you love me, you will wait for me.*

To these two women, and every woman reading *Getting to Know You*, you don't need to become frustrated, disappointed, or depressed when God is saving you from a lifelong ordeal of making the wrong choice or going down the wrong path. The cost of finding your way back is much more expensive than what you call a delay now.

Good news—before the completion of *Getting to Know You*, I received some positive news from Ann in Kenya. She is now engaged, surprisingly to a Luo man, even though before our most recent communication she had closed herself off to that possibility. She told me that my wise counsel helped her to look at differently at the man she ultimately married. Today she is happily married to what she calls "the best man in this world", a Luo man, and they have a beautiful daughter.

Francis & Nancy Kiogi, now Mr. & Mrs. Francis Kiogi from Navasha

CHAPTER 13

Oneness and One's Own Family

In Genesis 2:24, what do you think God meant by "A man shall leave his father and his mother"? Before a man is married, these are the two people most precious to him, his parents (father and mother). If you are a man, how will you obey this command without hurting your parents? And if you are a woman, how do you see yourself in a relationship where a man has left his parents for you? Do you keep him to yourself or learn to share him with his parents?

Never forget that your husband's parents will remain a part of his life forever. I would prefer that you and your husband make separate notes on this subject and later compare your notes. See where you agree on the ways the husband will leave his father and mother and cleave on to his wife, aiming to maintain a balance in sharing him with the parents so that no one feels offended or that the parents feel their son is being taken away from them. I know the challenges parents face when their son gets married. Again, with understanding, the family should become enlarged to contain everyone.

I would recommend you take time to read the book of Ruth in the Bible. In that book, there is a clear example of how to relate with a mother-in-law, namely the example of Ruth and Naomi. In fact, in the later part of the book, we find that Ruth was just like a daughter to her mother-in-law, who shared her concerns, worries, and interests. It was never a competition of taking away Naomi's son but of adding to the family. And that made them one.

Also we learn some lesions from the relationship of Naomi and her son-in-law Boaz. You can compare this relationship with that of Moses and his father-in-law, Jethro, and you can spot the difference. One was supportive, and the other was exploitative. It is important for a would-be couple to study these scriptures while dating so as to know both sides of the coin.

In the course of writing *Getting to Know You*, a friend asked me about the command for children to obey their parents, just as servants are to obey their masters and as we are to obey the government and our church leaders (Ephesians 6:1; Romans 13:1; Hebrews 13:17). However, the scriptures are clear that when a man marries, Christ becomes the husband's head, and the husband becomes the head of the wife (1 Corinthians 11:3). There is no confusion in the scriptures; we need to read them with understanding and wisdom.

You honour your parents because they are your parents, and you appreciate them for all they have done for you, but in your marriage, the arrangement changes from one of giving orders to one of advising, providing encouragement and assistance, and showing appreciation.

The relationship with your parents must change, from one of obedience to one of honour. You honour your parents because they are your parents, and you appreciate them for all they have done for you, but in your marriage, the arrangement changes from one of giving orders to one of advising, providing encouragement and assistance, and showing appreciation. Therefore, parents are not expected to go order their son on how he should live with his wife or organize his home. That is now left to the man and woman. Parents should be proud that their son is of age to marry and organize his home.

I had a personal experience in the early years of my marriage. My father was visiting from Nigeria, and he stayed with us. He saw all the things I was doing in the house, such as helping my wife in the kitchen, cooking, babysitting our daughter, washing and ironing our clothes, and sweeping the house. My father understands, based on his experience in Nigeria, that domestic work or household duties are left to the wife, meaning my wife in this case. In the first place, my wife is a working wife, leaving home at 6 a.m. to return at 4 p.m. Should there be an understanding on my part to assist with domestic work? Yes. I do this so as to release my wife from a hard day's work and give her time to rest. It also allows us all to have dinner together. Yes, as a journalist, I was able to work from home, so I was more flexible, and that made it possible for me to take care of the children and do some household chores. Is there anything wrong with a husband helping out his wife? No. Absolutely, it is encouraged.

I am home most of the time. Doing those chores was part of my daily routine; it was a normal day for me. It was not a burden, and it did not bring disrespect or disregard from my wife. As a matter of fact, she loved me more for it.

But there was a generational difference. In my dad's day, most of these things were assumed to be part of a wife's tasks in the house. Of course in his time in Nigeria, wives never worked but stayed home to take care of home matters. In our generation, we have learnt to share responsibilities in the house as husband and wife. It works for me in my home, so I don't want to change it. For my dad, he complained about it. Once I asked him to accept my decision and respect it. He soon discovered that neither my wife nor I had any problem helping out each other in the house. Do what is best for your marriage, what helps to make it work. Your parents should learn to back off when it comes to the administration of your home. Never compare your home with that of your children. You are a guest in their house; enjoy your stay so that you may be invited again. The same goes for the mother-in-law when she visits to assist the couple during childbearing experience. Do what you can, mothers-in-law, but don't try to run the home of your son and his wife.

I would pose some honest questions to both the man and woman to think about and talk about:

1. What challenges do you think you will have with your partner's family?
2. What challenges do you think you will have with your own family?
3. What principles can you and your partner come up with to guide your relationships with your extended families?
4. How will you handle your in-laws on both sides?
5. Will you have a preference for which of your parents will visit?

With this exercise, you begin to work together on how to improve your relationship with both families even before you enter into the marriage. Given the nature of this exercise, you will probably start discovering early enough the dos and don'ts in both families before you are married.

Never forget, you are marrying into two families—yours and that of your spouse.

Never forget, you are marrying into two families—yours and that of your spouse.

Titi & Loretta Godfrey wedding in Kisumu, Kenya

CHAPTER 14

Oneness of Vision

It is obvious that both man and woman have a different vision or visions before they come together in marriage. That includes a vision of what they think marriage is or what they expect in a marriage. During my counselling experiences of would-be couples, they were shocked at the question of what their vision was for their marriage. It is obvious that some visions are built on expectations rather than careful understanding of the plan of action for what to do in the marriage.

In this exercise, I want you again to separately, in the portion created, write down a list of four purposes you see for your marriage. You could do this in a notebook if you like. When you compare notes, remember that all these activities will be taking place before your wedding. I can assure you that if you complete this exercise, you will have a better understanding of marriage before you go into it. You will also get to know your partner better than ever. You cannot be lazy with planning for your wedding; it is a lifetime plan, so take your time to work on it. It will reflect years later on the type of marriage you have.

Your points regarding the purpose for marriage:

1	
2	
3	
4	

Your partner's point regarding the purpose for marriage:

1	
2	
3	
4	

Now compare your answers. You should have at least three points that are similar or closely resemble each other—if they're not the same, which is even better. Then pick those three points and break those points into goals.

I will illustrate what I mean so you may understand my explanation. If your expectation is to have children in the marriage, then having children is a good purpose.

Purpose 1: To have kids—the goal
How do you intend to achieve this?
Will you start a family immediately after wedding?
Will you wait one or two years after wedding?
How many kids do you intend to have in the family?
How will you space them, one or two years in between, or some other way?

Now set out the second purpose you have identified, along with the goals you intend to achieve from that purpose.

| Purpose 2 answer | |
| Purpose 3 answer | |

I expect that you have other purposes and goals in life in other areas of your life, such as church/ministry involvement, your vocation, your financial goals, your educational goals, and your goals for your extended family, among others.

From time to time during the courtship, get together with your partner to discuss the purposes and goals you have each identified. The quality time you spend on such discussions will guide you towards achieving the purposes and goals you have set for yourself when you finally get married. I personally made up my mind as a young man that I would love to have two children by God's grace no matter the circumstances in which I found myself. This decision was formed on the basis of providing for my children, wanting to give them the best of everything—love, attention, finances, and emotional support. When I met my partner, I shared this purpose with her, and I learnt she had similar purposes. We were in agreement in principle, even though we hadn't written anything down on paper, that we would have two children if we were eventually to marry each other. So far in our marriage, we have two beautiful daughters, although there has been family pressure on us, particularly from my family, and especially from my mother, to consider having another child, probably a son to make the family complete. I told my mom that the family is already complete.

My wife and I are pleased with our daughters. It was not difficult to handle such pressure from my family because Sandra and I are in agreement on our decision. A purpose agreed on from the very beginning is difficult to break. Even gossipers tried to put fear into my wife, saying that I would have a son out of wedlock or that I probably already had a son from another woman. Sandra was not bothered by this; she trusted me on my word. The truth is that we already had discussed this subject and had come to the understanding that we would be happy with whatever child or children God gave to us. It was not difficult for us to deal with the matter even when my mother took her case to my wife, thinking she would show better understanding as a woman. Sandra told my mom, "This is what your son wants, and I am OK with his decision." Whenever the family brings up the matter, we say in unison, "We are satisfied with the children God has given us. It was our conscious decision to have two." Once you have set your purpose and agreed upon it, the pressure is reduced. Now nobody talks about this issue any more, or if they do, they don't bring it to our attention. The girls themselves bring up the discussion once in a while and ask why they don't have a brother; many times they jokingly suggest that we give them a brother, and we say, "No problem. One will come soon," but they know we are joking about it. Sandra and I are satisfied with our daughters. We love our girls very much.

I must also inform you at this point that your purpose and goals may change, or you may reverse some purpose that is part of your family plan as time goes on. But whenever that happens, let it be done in the same manner we have previously used. Talk about it together, agree together about it, and implement the plan together.

Give God the freedom to revive, revisit, and rechannel your goals so they are in line with his purposes. For instance, I have always known I am called of God to be used for his kingdom or to work in the ministry, although I did not know how or when this would happen. When I met my partner, I was just a brother in the church. I shared with her the vision and revelations I had received years before. My purpose in doing so was to give her insight into my life. I asked her to pray about it so that she could fit into God's plans for my life.

Over the years, I have acquired more Christian education and have become ordained as a pastor with Victory Outreach International. I am more involved in ministry than when I met my partner, who is now my wife. Having a wife who is a career nurse—a very demanding profession with different working shifts—plus two children, I must plan properly to create a balance in our family. We don't have as much leisure time as we would like, but we have coped very well with all the changes we have undergone these past years, simply because we planned together and we are working on it together.

In 2006, I received a call from our church in the Netherlands to go on mission to Kenya. When I was asked, I could not simply say yes; I asked for time to talk it over with my wife. The request was granted. I spoke it over with my wife. After we prayed together about it, we both agreed it was a challenge worth undertaking for the Lord to fulfil his purpose for our lives. Some people were worried for us. We had young children, I had a business that was doing well, and my wife had a twelve-year career on the line. It was one of the easiest decisions we have made together because we were in tune with God on this matter even though many people tried to talk us out of it. I went back to the church leaders and confirmed our acceptance to go on the assignment to Kenya. Sandra and I were actually prepared for the long time it would take, so with all our personal effects, we left the Netherlands for Kenya with the intention to stay as long as the Lord desired us to be there.

Once I talked it over with Sandra, our minds were in agreement. She accepted to leave her career to go with me on mission as a helpmate and to support me in my calling to run the church. She would help with church administration and cater for our children's school needs. The decision to go to Kenya did not go down well with some of our family members and friends. On my wife's job, they tried to persuade her not to go, hoping to talk her out of it, asking her to stay behind with the children since she had a stable job and a salary.

They suggested she could be of financial support to me in the ministry in Kenya, which was true. As true as that sounded, our being together was more important to us than money. Also, people were worried about our children's schooling; the language challenge, moving from Dutch to English; housing; our security; and our safety.

We honestly considered all these factors, and we decided to do all we could to assist our children in adjusting to Kenya and enjoying their stay there. After five years with the children in Kenya, they loved it so much and wanted us to stay on, but we had to return to the Netherlands once we had completed our task in Kenya. Till this day, they ask, "When are we going back to Kenya?" On a personal level, it was a life-changing experience, and I would do it all over again if the opportunity ever emerges. I was challenged in all areas of my life, but I saw faith in action. I never knew the simple decision of going to Kenya on mission would have made such an impact on my life, one that remains to this day.

On a personal note, I had a flourishing magazine, *The Voice*, which I had nurtured for seven years as of 2006. I had to leave it behind in the hands a new management team to answer the call of God. Was it difficult for me to let go of my business where I had a stable income and to move into a situation where I had to depend on a church support? Yes it was. But we trusted in the one who had called us—God. On the other hand, as I mentioned earlier, we never gave a second thought to the decision to go to Kenya and to leave our lives in the Netherlands behind to fulfil God's purpose upon our lives. Since it was a sacrifice made by my wife and children, I truly did my best to make sure they lacked nothing in Kenya such as food, shelter, and security.

I can tell you that the decision to go to Kenya affected all aspects of our lives, including our finances, our relationships, and our contact with our families, but the most important thing to me and Sandra was that we were together in our decision. We survived the stay in Kenya and returned peacefully to Europe when our task was accomplished. Our marriage is intact, and our children have done well in their growth and their studies. Both of them are now in higher institutions of learning. They gained a great deal of confidence in facing life's challenges from their experience in Kenya.

Test

Your Family's Goals

As of _____ [date]

Goals (Do not include aspects of your wedding plan here)	Current plan of action needed	Timeline for the goal to be achieved	Financial requirements	Date intended to achieve the goal	
Current goals					
Long-term goals					
Future goals					

CHAPTER 15

Children—the Fruit of Oneness

In many courtships, when the subject on children, the couple prefer to defer the matter, often postponing talking about it until after their wedding. I say it is advisable to talk about it now, before you are married, so as to give you both an idea of what you want or desire together in your union, of course never forgetting that it is God who grants the favour to have children. Also, what happens if you can't have children? Do you stay together and continue to love one another, resolving to consider other opportunities available to you as a couple?

Never forget that the two shall become one, both in body (flesh) and in spirit; you are no longer going to be alone. Whatever affects one person in the marriage automatically affects the other person. I hear people say, "But what if it is the fault of the man [or the woman] that the couple can't have a child?" Well, that is why you are one now; because what affects one also affects the other. Therefore, the solution is in your resolution to walk through it together and not engage in a blame game. If it is true that one of you is unable to have children, then I recommend that you work together on the problem, rather than abandon the other person. I have encountered couples who have problems conceiving for years; they have tried everything they'd been advised to do by medical professionals, and yet there is still no solution. If you are in such a situation, sit together and talk about it. You have other options open and available to you such as adoption. The procedure varies from country to country. I am not using *Getting to Know You* to promote adoption, but if it turns out that you need to adopt, there is nothing wrong with such a decision. Both of you should agree and do it together.

The child is going to be your child; you are to be father and mother to the child. I have guided some parents on this path, and today they are happy with their children. I have some children in my family today who were adopted, and they have blended fully with my biological children. We are one big happy family.

Whatever affects one person in the marriage automatically affects the other person.

On the matter of the number of children you should have in the family, I would suggest that you go for the number of children you believe you can adequately cater for considering your resources and all your other circumstances. Take care of your body; don't make children for the sake of having children, except if God decides to bless you with more. I have a friend who had two sets of twins (girls) three times, meaning he has six children. He and his wife decided to make one more child, and they were hoping for a boy. That was the prayer request they brought before God, and God granted them their request and tripled the blessing. The woman gave birth to three sons in addition to the six girls she'd already had, so suddenly there were nine children in the family. Well, as good as the new additions were to the family, it brought stress upon the man and woman, both financially and emotionally, as they sought to provide the best for them. According to the man, he had to completely stop coming close to his wife for fear of making more children. Despite the additional joy to the family, it really stressed the whole family, including the older girls, to look after three sons at the same time. They had gone to seek medical advice, and thereafter they lived with having to care for the nine children. Still it is important for you to plan your family. Do not expect that God will provide for your children after you have given birth to them.

I know the challenge is that some people want to have children of both sexes—male and female. What is wrong if you are blessed with a child of one particular sex? I have two daughters, and if I want to have a male child, I will be forced to have more children. But who guarantees me that the next child will be a boy? What if I have a daughter again? Therefore, the gender of your child shouldn't be a problem, because you are not the one to determine the sex of your children. Medically, the man determines the sex of the child, so what you deposit is what you get back. Rather than blame a woman for giving you only girls or boys, accept the children and enjoy them. As a result of having one particular gender of children, either boys or girls, many parents intend to go on having more children, but this is not advisable, particularly in the times we live in. The social system is getting smaller, so it no longer supports large families.

Another family friend was attempting to have a male child; they had five girls, but one of the parents still was not satisfied; in the end they had six daughters and one son. Now they have a very large family, and taking care of all the children has taken its toll on the marriage, the couple's resources, and their relationship. They no longer have time for each other, being busy each day catering for the children, which is enough work for the whole year. What the family is experiencing today is the blame game: "You caused it." "No, you did." It is a collective error of judgement because none of us is the one who determines the sex of our children. It is God who gives children. You should be prepared and pleased to accept what God gives to you as a couple.

With my two adorable daughters, at no time have I ever complained to my wife that she couldn't give me a male child. Nor have I blamed myself for being too lazy to have a male child. In African society, a man who has no male child is viewed as lazy. I don't know where such an idea comes from. I guess from the pit of hell. I am happy with my girls, and I pray they become successful in life and live in good health with sound minds. I am not lazy. My wife will attest to that. For us, a child is a child. What is important is to treat the children the same way and give them equal opportunities in life. I don't see much difference between a boy child and a girl child.

The myth that a male child will care for you when you get older or retired is not something that is guaranteed. I have seen many families where the girl child has been the supportive arm of the family, providing even for the men. Also, I do not need a child to succeed me and continue my name, I am a person, and I live as a person; I am not reproducing myself in my children. I want my children to be themselves, have their own identities, and fulfil their destinies as God has a destiny for each of them.

The would –be-couple need to answer the following questions prayerfully, then together reach such agreements as:

- How many children do we sense God would like us to have?
  Answer:

- How will we space them, or will we let God give them without any planning on our part?
  Answer:

In my parents' time, children weren't something that a couple considered ahead of time, with a few exceptions. The children just came as the Lord wished. I still wonder how my parents were able to take care of us eight children under one roof with one bedroom and one sitting room. I look back and say it was a miracle we all survived. Today each of my children has a room to themselves, and I have a three-bedroom house, so if I have four children, where would I get extra rooms for them? Things have changed. We should understand the times we live in and plan accordingly.

One of my uncles had four wives and several children. He counted only the male children, numbering fourteen, and the girls didn't matter much to him because they would soon go their own separate ways in marriage. If you feel God would have you plan your family, then research, pray, and decide together on what family planning methods you intend to use as the family grows.

(It is important that this is agreed upon from the beginning to avoid accidental pregnancy after you have stopped having children.) I never subscribe to abortion, so if it turns out you become pregnant, then you have to carry the pregnancy to term and bear the child. Health-wise, if you have stopped childbirth for a period of time and you are ageing, it is dangerous for you suddenly to become pregnant again. You need medical supervision for a safe delivery.

Be sure that the method or methods you choose are not abortive in nature, because you could be committing murder in an attempt to stop yourself or your wife from being pregnant again. If you abort a pregnancy, it does not matter at what stage; it would be committing murder, which is sin against God. You don't want to sin against God in your marriage.

The whole idea of family planning is to keep the sperm of the man from reaching the egg of the woman; when that happens, the result is pregnancy and the beginning of the process of life. If the sperm and the egg meet and fertilization occurs, and if the egg is kept from developing in the uterus, you have aborted it. It is that simple, so avoid this temptation. The consequence of such an action is a *sin* against God.

A married pastor, after several years of taking a break from childbearing, suddenly discovered that his wife had missed her period. They knew the consequence, so they sought for my advice.

I simply told them congratulations. Today they have new addition to their family, a son. Since I have touched on this, I need to bring to your attention the subject of adoption again. I mentioned earlier that you can go for the option of adopting a child from the country of your choice. Many African countries and other places around the world have good adoption policies. Once you meet the requirements, it will be possible to adopt a child.

It is God who gives children. You should be prepared and pleased to accept what God gives to you as a couple.

How Do You Currently Feel about Adoption?

A beautiful couple, well-to-do, joined our church in 2009 in Kenya. They had a medical challenge, having been informed that it was practically impossible for them to have a child biologically. They had received treatment, had sought prayers, and had waited for four years into their marriage. Despite their faith in God, they still had no result after waiting some years more, so they decided to adopt a young baby (a boy). They had been visiting an orphanage when they spotted the young lad; both the man and the woman fell in love with the child. They discussed the possibilities of his adoption with the management of the orphanage, and they were given the green light. They drove back home. They prayed about it and decided that they would do through with the adoption. It was not to make one person happy; it was the joint decision of both parents. However, when they returned to discuss the matter with their local church pastor, he kicked it to the ground, saying that they should wait upon the Lord. They felt disappointed as they had waited for years and had been told it was not medically possible for them to have a child together. They came to see me for a second opinion. My advice, after they had settled into our church, was to ask them some questions. My first question to them was if they loved the child or if they just wanted to adopt a child to satisfy the shame of not having one of their own. The only reason they should adopt, I felt, was if they loved the child enough to have him as a part of their lives and their family. They replied, "Yes." I gave them my blessing and assisted them with a recommendation letter as capable parents for adopting the child and caring for the child. Under Kenyan laws, without such a trusted recommendation, you are not qualified and are not allowed to put in an application for child adoption no matter the circumstances. This couple needed to process the adoption papers, but they continually went to visit the baby and spend time with him. The boy became fun for them. When the adoption papers were ready, the boy was seven years old. He has lived with the couple ever since. Now he is a young boy, having grown up to know this couple as his parents. They are all one family. God has provided him a beautiful home and loving parents. If you did not know the situation, you would see no sign that he is adopted. He is welcome and loved by the parents.

Let me also address some myths that often bring conflicts within the African marriage environment:

What Procedure Will You Use in Naming Your Children?

Many people place a lot of significance on the naming of a child. For instance, in many African societies, children are named by grandparents, if they are still alive, or the grandparents suggest names. With Christianity and other religious views, names are given in accordance with the family's faith and belief. For us as Christians, the majority of our names are culled from the Holy Bible. It is important you also secure the meaning of the names you choose. Either the man or the woman can suggest a name, but let it be that you agree together before giving the name and before the general public knows it. It is appropriate that the husband announce the name simply as the head of the family. It should be the name you have agreed on for your child. Let there be no surprises of a new name just because you like the name, without discussing it with your spouse.

What will be the first name, the second name, and of course the family name? In Kenyan culture, I noticed that many married couples do not bear the family name of the husband. In many other cultures, it is a matter of choice. A woman may bear her maiden name even after marriage, and therefore the children may bear the name of their mother. Since you as a couple are one, it is appropriate that everything in the family be one. Give uniform names, and bear a common name with your spouse. I know it creates much confusion when children bear different family names; in fact, outside Africa, such a practice is not acceptable. You have to show proof of a family connection where the names are different, especially if the name is on the birth certificate.

All births are registered immediately after the child is delivered in Europe, for instance; therefore, you must have the names ready for the midwife to register your child in a central database after birth. Such names may not be changed or altered after they are registered. I know a family where the couple do not agree on the name for their son. The wife says the child's name is one thing, whereas the man gives another name. Every time you mention the name of the child, it causes a quarrel between the husband and wife, with one saying "That is not the name I gave him" or the other one saying "That is not his name." Finally it was decided that the boy would bear both names to appease the parents. So talk about it before the baby arrives. Make a selection of names, and pick the one you find most appealing to both of you. If, for instance, the children do not bear common family name, then their rightful position is denied because of mistakes or carelessness in names given to the children.

My family name is Iruh; all my children, including my adopted children, bear Iruh as their last name. If, for instance, any of them choose to bear my first name, Elvis, they may not be able to prove that they are an Iruh or that Elvis is one and the same person. Give your children uniform family names. It is very important.

Who Will Discipline the Children?

Discipline, yes. From time to time, as the child begins to grow, discipline needs to occur and needs to be applied in the family as one unit. In fact, it is proven that children divide their parents along emotional lines when there is no agreement on who should discipline the children. My wife and I often agree on what type of discipline is to be meted out to our kids. Discipline includes denying them access to watching television or their favourite programme, and having them clean their rooms, make their beds, wash the dishes, sweep the house, run errands, and do their school assignments on time. Discipline here does not include using corporal discipline on kids, such as caning. I have learnt from experience not to hit my children with my bare hands; rather, I speak to them constantly. Once there is no disagreement on who will discipline the kids, there will be oneness and orderliness in the family. The children will respect your decisions faster and quicker.

How and Where Will the Children Be Disciplined?

Start early, as soon as they are able to speak few words, with talking to them and instructing them.

The discipline should start from your home, not outside the home, because then it may simply be too late. Let the children understand that you and your spouse behave as one and that you are in agreement in all things. Communicate with them clearly and correctly at home. Make sure they understand what you mean by discipline. My wife and I don't raise our hands to discipline our children, and you shouldn't do that either. Talk with your eyes and hands, giving signs and showing reactions, but do not hit your children with your hands. If you do, they will become fearful—and that gives rise to another problem: they distance themselves from you or become even more rebellious. A simple look gives my daughters my message; the same is true with their mother. Before we go out of the house for an event or occasion, we brief our children on what we expect of them in terms of behaviour and conduct. They do break our rules once in a while. At those times, we discipline them when we get back home. Let all discipline be carried out in love. The kids are so loved that we discipline them.

We teach our children to apologize when they do something wrong and also to say sorry when they have done things wrong. It is beautiful to see this in a family, and it is possible to achieve. Be disciplined yourself as parents. My wife and I cannot afford to quarrel and fight before the children and then expect them to accept discipline from the same parents. In such a situation, it is tough to achieve discipline, so work on your personal relationship and your conduct before you start with your children.

Will You Have House Help?

In most Western societies, childcare is not a problem as working parents have various arrangements for their young children: kindergarten, day-care centres, Head Start, and organized home caretakers for children under four years of age. However, in many African societies, the hiring of house help is still optional. I don't personally have anything against having house help, but the danger is that many of the house help are not very well educated and these young children are left to their care. You need to properly train your help so that they don't have your baby poisoned or not properly cared for during your absence. Not too long ago, a video went viral on the Internet showing a woman—house help—in Uganda abusing a baby in her care, beating the baby mercilessly without any form of provocation from the baby. Her act was simply evil. But again, how many children left in the hands of house help have been treated in such a manner? The babies cannot report the abuse except if there are physical marks or bruises on the child, but the sociological effect on the child is damaging. Many of the working parents are gone the whole day, so it is obvious that the children are left in the care of others. Both the husband and the wife need to agree on the type of house help—a live-in who stays with them, or a work-and-go arrangement where the help comes in the morning and then leaves in the evening when the couple returns. Those who do not choose the house help option decide that the wife stays home to look after the children. If financially the family can cope with one salary, then the wife looking after the kids is just perfect for the upbringing of the children.

Sometimes family begins to observe strange behaviour from their children, and they wonder the source. Most of the time it is from the house help; bad behaviour and bad habits are copied from the house help. If you need to have a house helper, you must clearly and understandably make him or her know what role he or she is to play in the lives of your children. For instance, will he or she be allowed to discipline the child or children in your absence, and if so, to what extent? You need to watch that he or she does not maltreat your children in your absence or bully them into a state of fear to the point that they can no longer express themselves. I prefer that you decide what is suitable in your circumstance for your children. It should always be in the best interests of the children.

Will Extended Family Be Involved in Your Marriage?

Will extended family members stay with you? If yes, who and at what stage? This may be less important to you, but it could bring stress upon the young marriage with other persons involved, particularly family members, at the very early stage. If you have no urgent need, such as taking care of young children or attending to a medical condition, you should learn to live together as a couple. In fact, the early stage of your marriage should not be shared with someone else, not even your parents. Politely ask them to give you room so you may get to know each other and understand each other better. In the past, the bride was given a young maiden (a girl) to assist her in the marriage, but in many cases, the wife ends up being busier with the help than with her husband. You soon hear comments such as, "I didn't ask for a second wife." The danger of extended family living with you at the beginning also has to do with how you expect them to relate with your wife or husband or even your children. Do they also discipline your children? Will they be allowed to discipline the children? If so, how?

Educational Goals for Your Children

Even though this is a long-term projection, there is nothing wrong in discussing it as early as possible as the child or children grow. When I was a kid growing up, my father placed a strong emphasis on education. He didn't have educated parents, but through a family member, he was taken to the city, where he furthered his education. Later on in life, he paid for his own studies. His emphasis on education was total. He was not prepared to tolerate any child who did not want an education. He was concerned that all his children must have a good education so that we could support ourselves in the future. My mother, on the other hand, had a lesser education. She did not place so much emphasis on education, but she supported the idea that her children should be educated, so both parents were in agreement on education. From Mama, we would get some encouragement with regards to our education, but according to Dad, education was not optional. Education was compulsory. But then I could not participate in other activities such as playing football, which I really liked. For my dad, doing sports was waste of time. Just study your books and pass your examinations with good grades.

"All study and no play makes Jack a dull boy." There must be a balance with education and other curriculum activities such as sports. There needs to be an agreement and a collective effort to ensure the children get the right education. Where would you like them to go to school? Would they go to a boarding school or a day school? How will you handle kids who are not academically inclined but who are very good with other talents and craftsmanship? How will you handle children who are gifted and who attend a special school? Children like this will demand special attention with their studies. Will you have time for the children's education? If you adequately prepare for these things, it won't come as a surprise to you, catching you in an unprepared state.

With our move to Kenya, Sandra and I knew the children would demand extra attention for their studies. They were born in the Netherlands; they spoke and wrote Dutch perfectly well; but they now had to learn in English and adapt very fast to the new academic environment. Although young, they needed our help to adjust and cope with the change so they did not get discouraged. I had to help them more because of the English language. While we were in Holland, their mom helped them more with their studies because then their education was delivered in the Dutch language. The responsibility automatically fell on me in Kenya to help our daughters with their education because of the change of the language of instruction to English. We accepted to help with our children's education.

You and your spouse must be willing to complement each other when it comes to your children's education. You must show interest and concern in everything related to their education. When the children have school functions, which parent will attend? Or will you go together? Never allow it to become a pattern that both parents are too busy to attend any of the school functions with the children. It is proven that children who have parents attend their school functions develop better confidence in dealing with academic issues. Many times I was with the girls for swimming lessons, or both my wife and I were there to share their victories or encourage them when they had not done so well in school competitions. Always one of us parents is around to share the experience with the children.

Who Will Help the Children with Homework from School?

I am very poor in arithmetic or mathematics; therefore, I've never tried to help my kids with these subjects. Their mother does that, while I provide help with English, social studies, geography, history, and general knowledge. When we returned to Holland, I couldn't help my children with the Dutch language. My Dutch is not good, so I left that with my wife while I worked with my children on their English-language skills, a balance for them. I didn't want to spoil their knowledge of the Dutch language. Outsiders do not see this weakness because my wife and I work together as a team in all aspects of our children's education. We agreed at the very beginning what we would do with their education and at what level we would do it.

What Are Your Individual Goals for Your Children?

(List them in any order here.)

Once you and your spouse are in agreement, arrange the list in order of priority with the most important goals first. Remember, this is to be done before you have kids. When you have your children, review your agreed goals; consider if they are still viable or if you need to make amendments or set new goals. These decisions should rest between husband and wife in the interests of your family. Depending on whether you have a boy or a girl, the goals you have set out may change.

How will you handle children who are gifted in areas other than academics but who struggle with academic schoolwork?

The tips mentioned in *Getting to Know You* come from the real experiences of couples who have shared their stories with me. Some of these issues were not probably dealt with, and they later came to haunt the marriage. Children are the blessings of God, a joy and not a burden to both parents. When you have children is not the time for blame games and name-calling: "You're a dull head like your mother" or "You're lazy like your father." The mother of your children is your darling wife. Why did you marry her if she was such a dull head? Or why did you marry your husband if he is such a lazy man? There must be some good qualities you saw; hold on to those beautiful qualities. Agree on what to do, such as encouraging your children whenever possible, rather than pulling them down or bullying them to be like the other children. Approach parenting together. Let your child know that he or she has the support of you as the parents.

One young girl, at twelve years old, was already playing pranks with her studies. Although she was not academically good, she did her best, and her teachers tried to help her, but she was a slow learner and had trouble understanding academic work, and she was struggling to catch up with her classmates. After she had twice repeated primary four, her classmates were already in secondary school. Her father gave up on her and not only that, but also she was constantly bullied with abusive words at home. The mother tried to encourage her, but since it was not coming from both parents, it was not effective. Finally the girl ran away from home and joined a gang of bad girls. She ended up in prostitution. Years later, she turned from that ugly lifestyle to pursue a skills-training career in fashion design and tailoring, where she has succeeded in putting her life back on course. She regrets her wasteful years. If only her parents had understood that she had other options to learn a skill if she did not do well at her studies.

Her parents did not understand her and did not help her out of her predicament. If the child is not academically strong, encourage him or her to learn a skill. The basic education of primary or secondary school is enough. Let him or her learn a trade or a skill so he or she may be confident and have a purposeful approach to life.

Who Will Attend School Functions?

This is another aspect of children's lives. They need the involvement of their parents on the prize-giving day, for instance, or for a drama club performance, a school musical performance, or a group singing competition, among other such activities. Depending on the working schedule of both parents, one should be available to attend to the child's or children's needs at school. In my personal experience, my kids are always joyous when one of us is able to attend the school concert, the parents' meeting, the assessment gathering, etc. If you can avoid assigning such tasks to your family members or helpers/maids, it will be better. It helps to improve relationship and to encourage the involvement of all concerned in the family. It keeps the family as a unit.

The same thing goes for the children's homework from school. Let one parent be available to assist the child with schoolwork. I know how difficult this has become in our modern society where the father and mother are both working parents. Do your best to be the last person who sees the school assignment or homework of your children. Let them feel your love enough that you show interest in their schoolwork and you are involved too, even if it is for a few minutes each day before they go to bed.

Help where you can with corrections as well. My youngest daughter always wanted me to help her by correcting her work. She trusted my answers to be correct. Even when her mother did this job, I presented my corrections to my daughter. Now she is in the university. Always the family must be committed to teamwork when it comes to the children's education.

CHAPTER 16

Physical Oneness

They were naked and not ashamed.

—Genesis 2:25

Physical oneness is totally reserved by God for married couples *only*. This means there is to be no moving into physical oneness until you are pronounced husband and wife either in a civil, traditional, or religious ceremony. Then you are allowed to share intimacy between one another (a man and a woman). This type of relationship involves being naked before one another and yet not ashamed. Can you imagine seeing the nakedness of someone other than your spouse? It is not a pleasant view except you are of corrupt mind.

Have you thought why we place so much emphasis on that first kiss? In essence, that is supposed to be the first oneness between a man and a woman after they have exchanged their vows, and after they've been blessed and witnessed by a crowd of people, so therefore no one will accuse them of violating God's idea of marriage. Should we not then kiss before marriage? *Yes*, but not lip-to-lip kissing. You should not do anything that brings the type of closeness that could be compared to oneness, such as kissing with mouths touching, touching of the body, and embracing each other for so long that you start developing other forms of feelings. This is to guide against temptation.

Men, how many other women have you kissed whom you weren't married to—if the kissing was allowed? Have you actually had physical oneness with these women given the fact that you have kissed them? If you have kissed women who are not your wife, then you should ask for forgiveness. You may have done it out of ignorance, but it is no excuse. And if you have not done it, then you now know better.

Physical oneness is totally reserved by God for married couples *only*.

However, even in marriage, physical oneness can be hindered by a number of things, which I intend to address. In recent years, over a period of three to four decades, new sexually transmitted diseases (STDs), including the common STDs such chlamydia, genital warts, herpes, gonorrhoea, hepatitis, and syphilis, came into limelight, and also including the fearsome HIV/AIDS.

The question is, how do you deal with these things mostly from your past life, before you came to the knowledge of Christ? If you suffer from any of these aforementioned diseases, it could affect your oneness with your spouse-to-be. If that is the case, take proper medical treatment and inform your spouse-to-be of this situation before your wedding. Seek medical counselling and deal with the problem together.

Following are some of the more common issues in love relationships which should be addressed:

1. The Urge to Hide Things from Your Spouse-to-Be, Surprising Him or Her Later with Such Information

I would expect that before you make any commitment to your partner, you should be truthful about your medical situation or condition. If you already know of any medical information that may hamper your marriage, it is wise and advisable to disclose it. Don't keep it as a secret to be revealed after the wedding. I also suggest that you get reliable medical tests done to ascertain your status.

Where there are challenges, you should agree on a plan on how to handle them and then commit to any medical treatment or medications recommended. Your doctor or counsellor will be happy to talk to you about any continuing fears you have in the area of STIs including HIV/AIDS. I have had several cases of such people, who had also been given advice by other pastors. It is not in our power to give people false hope. Don't encourage one HIV-infected person to wed a person who is not infected on the grounds that God will heal the other person! What if God chooses not to heal the person? The medical implications then are very complicated. Some families, on religious grounds, have gone ahead to wed, then within a period of two years, the wife also died. In one such case, the only daughter from the marriage was also infected with the virus, and she died at just one year of age. The man eventually was infected as well and had to live with the consequences of his naive actions. Do not be fooled, such advice is suicidal; so all persons need to be careful when it comes to this subject. There is nothing wrong with taking a blood test to determine your status before wedding. In fact, I say this should be done before the engagement, as early as possible in the relationship. It is not a cause for shame. And do not hide your status from your partner, no matter the outcome of the test result. Those who didn't know they were infected before they were married, there is medical assistance so the couple may have kids who are HIV-free and can live a normal life.

Also people with blood deficiencies, such as sickle-cell anaemia, commonly referred to as SS, are advised not to wed a person with the same gene for SS. The danger is that the possibility of transferring the gene to their children is very high, and therefore it is risky for these two people to have children. I am not a medical person, but I have put together some information for you on sickle-cell anaemia. I am told it is a common disease among people from tropical climates such as Africa. Sickle-cell anaemia is the most common form of sickle-cell disease (SCD). SCD is a serious blood disorder in which the body makes sickle-shaped red blood cells. "Sickle-shaped" means that the red blood cells are shaped like a crescent. It must be said that normal red blood cells are disc-shaped and look like doughnuts without holes in the centre. They move easily through the blood vessels. Red blood cells contain an iron-rich protein called haemoglobin. This protein carries oxygen from the lungs to the rest of the body.

Sickle cells contain abnormal haemoglobin called sickle haemoglobin or haemoglobin S. Sickle haemoglobin causes the cells to develop a sickle, or crescent, shape. Sickle cells are stiff and sticky. They tend to block blood flow in the blood vessels of the limbs and organs. Blocked blood flow can cause pain and organ damage. It can also raise the risk for infection.

Sickle-cell anaemia has no widely available cure. Ultimately, on many occasions, the carrier often dies prematurely. However, treatments to improve the anaemia and the lesser complications can help with the symptoms and complications of the disease in both children and adults. The most helpful treatment is blood and marrow stem cell transplant, which may offer a cure for a small number of people.

Over the past hundred years, doctors have learnt a great deal about sickle-cell anaemia. They know its causes, how it affects the body, and how to treat many of its complications. Therefore, it is advisable not to wed a person with SS if you also have SS or even AS, as the risk of your children being afflicted with this blood disorder is very high.

Sickle-cell anaemia varies from person to person. Some people who have the disease have chronic (long-term) pain or fatigue (tiredness). However, with proper care and treatment, many people who have the disease can have improved quality of life and reasonable health much of the time.

Because of improved treatments and care, people who have sickle-cell anaemia are now living into their forties or fifties, or even longer. But why take the risk when you have the right information at your disposal? Get to know your blood types before making serious lifetime commitments.

2. Fear of Past Sins Being Revealed

All past relationships *must* be brought to the light, first with your pastor as a confidant, then with your partner, with whom you should deal with it through counselling. If you have difficulty with this issue, you may be helped.

Should you share only the basics? This has nothing to do with you confessing to your partner as if you are sinning currently. It is something from the past to deal with, and if you feel led to deal with it, then please go ahead. The person who deserves all confession is God; ask him for forgiveness through your prayers. You must not hide anything from God even though he knows all. Confessing these past relationships will kill your fear of the past being revealed later since you have revealed it yourself. Your confession will also deal a blow to guilt, blame, shame, and maybe even any bitterness you have against yourself.

While I was working on *Getting to Know You*, an incident happened in the United States. It was widely reported in the media that a couple who had been married for just four days had broken up the marriage. And then the husband had gone and strangled the wife to death. Why? He had discovered that his newly wedded wife had had an affair with his best friend, and he was never told of the affair until four days after his wedding. Why didn't she mention it before it was discovered? The guilt, the hurt, the pain, and the anger would have been dealt with even if it meant that the relationship was broken. But her failure to disclose the relationship had a fatal consequence.

Never say that a past affair is no longer important. If it is not dealt with, it very well may come back to hurt the marriage and the people involved. The irony of it all is that when you keep such a secret, you give your spouse reason not to trust you again. Whatever else you are keeping away from your spouse-to-be is better revealed now. Although I must say that this man's action was extreme. One doesn't have to kill to correct a wrong. For no reason can you justify killing someone, no matter the circumstance, even if you encounter a circumstance as severe as the one just described.

3. Memories of a Past Relationship

Where there has been abuse such as rape or forceful carnal knowledge that may not be rape (sexual acts engaged in against one's wishes, or incest), your pastor and his wife or a godly counsellor can walk you through the process of bringing it into the light. Forgiving and being set free are both very important. These are issues you must deal with before starting a new relationship and definitely before talking of wedding. I have in my few years of pastoring discovered how difficult it is to talk about this subject, particularly rape or incest. It is such an abomination, especially for a woman, who often blames herself for what has been done to her as if it is her fault—or people in society blame her for what has happened to her. Therefore, many people want to keep such things a secret and they do not talk about it. But such a woman may find it difficult to relate with a man when it comes to sexuality in the marriage and being open to one another. Some women become self-protective and even dress to protect themselves in their own homes for fear of being raped again, no matter that a woman in such a predicament is alone with her husband in the house. If you talk to a professional counsellor, you need to let both your pastor and your partner know what you are going through and the basis of the problem. Again, your partner must show restraint so that you don't allow the incident to become a stage for revenge or jealousy in you or your partner to the extent that it would lead you to sin against God.

Be very prayerful about the situation, knowing that revealing such information releases you from the fear that your spouse-to-be may find out. God has given me a gift in this area to help people who have gone through such experiences. Today, the people I have counselled in this area have been set free and are enjoying their married lives.

Note that where there has been sexual abuse in the past, the partner will need to be very sensitive and caring in the process of healing if the couple are to become one again. Your partner's love life can be rebuilt with time where trust has been destroyed. In that aspect, trust in the beginning may be difficult, but if you sincerely help one another, your sex life will even become more enjoyable. Hopefully going through *Getting to Know You* will help you deal positively with this issue, which sometimes comes up in marriages, so that it does not negatively affect your physical oneness.

4. Comparison to Past Relationships

If there is any action that you must avoid in your relationship as you walk towards wedding or once you are already married, it would be the act of bringing your past relationship into your new relationship. A previous relationship should not be the yardstick you use to measure what you have now, seeing it as either better or worse than your previous relationship. Never, never do this, or else you will kill the relationship before it even starts. If your first relationship or some other past relationship was so good, why are you no longer in it? Whatever happened in your past relationship was not as good as what you have now? Let it go and forget about it. You must register that in your mind and apply it. I have seen a partner argue about how a previous partner treated him or her. "How nice he was! And he was so good to me." Why, then, are you no longer with him or her? Your new partner is not your former partner, so it would not make any difference talking about your previous partner with your current partner. The same applies for the man. Don't draw comparison between your ex-girlfriend and your current partner, even when it is meant to be a joke. It is too expensive a joke to crack in your relationship.

Treat what you have now as the best and as if nothing else exists to you. No partner wishes to be compared to someone else. Can you imagine sleeping beside your partner once you are married as he or she is calling out the name of her or his ex-partner?

I read a story of a couple where, on the night in question, the man was tired and just turned his back towards his wife to go to sleep. The wife began to think of all sorts of things: *Maybe my husband is seeing another woman. Maybe I am no longer attractive to him. Maybe he is angry with me.* Both of them slept the night apart. The next morning, the husband said to the wife, "I am so disappointed that last night my favourite football team, Arsenal, lost again. I lost my appetite even for my food, to the extent that I just went to bed."

So it was nothing about the wife or another woman but about a football game—and yet the wife's head was already full of ideas and she couldn't get to sleep.

If you are not clear about something, talk it over with your partner—and don't assume that what you are thinking is what the problem is. His or her mind may just be far away from such thoughts, bothered with other issues of life. Do away with all your old relationships, which never ended up in a marriage, and don't bring them into your new relationship. Even gift items that remind you of your past relationship should be dispensed with before tying the knot with the new partner.

5. Guilt over Past Relationships

You are living in guilt if you are wishing you were still with your former partner. The danger of guilt is that it shows in your words and actions. You were a very caring person before, but because of your guilt, you are now reserved. You talk less and relate less with your partner. Not talking much and being fearful of exposing yourself to your new partner will create a complex issue in your marriage. You are afraid of being vulnerable. Seek counsel with your pastor if you continue to feel guilty over a past relationship. Don't keep quiet about it, saying, "It will heal with time." Time never heals a wound unless you deal with the wound. Other issues related to guilt that need to be addressed include anger or bitterness towards the opposite sex because of your past experiences. Sometimes I hear women say, "I hate men"—yet the person you are going to wed is a man. How are you going to love him when you hate men? Your husband is a reminder of all men. You have to deal with your painful memories of sexual abuse or any other issue attached to it. I hear women say that because of the sexual abuse, they no longer have a sexual urge or any interest in sex, yet in marriage the two partners have to satisfy each other sexually. Then the fear of rejection by your spouse, if he does not know of your situation, creeps in; coldness, hurt, worry, and lack of communication in your marriage are signs that you have closed yourself up and you need help urgently. Many times sexual problems are usually symptoms of other problems in the marriage which have not been dealt with and which are carried over into our marriage.

6. Inability to Communicate

In many African societies, sex is not spoken about; it just happens. It can be difficult to talk about sex. But I break that traditional and cultural curse in Jesus's name, and I release you to talk about it now and always. How come you can talk about every other thing except sex in your marriage? Let each other know what you feel for each other. Start doing this the very first night of your marriage. Don't postpone it for another day or until after your honeymoon. Why are you having a honeymoon then? This part is why you have been longing to get married, so why not enjoy your sex life? By God's ordinance you are permitted to enjoy sex with your wife. Your honeymoon is not a business trip; its purpose is that you enjoy one another in open intimacy for the first time and for the rest of your lives. Marriage is not a talk show, or a life of work and sleep! Now enjoy your new friendship approved by God in marriage. Let each other know what you want. What does not feel good? God expects us to enjoy our marriage. If I were counselling you, I would give you specific details on how to please your spouse. Experiencing oneness, as with everything else that is important and precious in a marriage, is sacred. It takes a lot of time and work to get it right. Don't get frustrated and give up. Try to improve this area of your married life. Read, learn, ask your spouse questions, listen, and share. You are one now, so never forget that you should be able to talk over everything to improve your oneness. Men and women are *very* different from person to person. For this reason, avoid going to a third party to discuss your sex life with your wife or husband. I have heard of a married man going to complain to a single woman about how boring his sex life is. If you do such a thing, you are inviting trouble into your marriage. Before you know it, the single woman is after your marriage and is lusting after you.

Don't copy what others do in their homes; it may not work for you. Find out what works for you in your home, and apply it in your marriage. It is impossible to know how your spouse is feeling and what he or she is thinking unless you are willing to talk about it with him or her. Let him or her know how you feel. Become good talkers and good listeners. And be joyous with one another as often as possible.

1 Corinthians 7:1–5 gives further instructions in this area, including the limitation on how being physically apart from each other is possible. Given the amount of time you spend in prayer and fasting, it is clear that God's purpose is that husbands and wives live together and meet each other's needs. This will require sacrifices, but his grace and provision will be there for you.

Do not neglect your relationship. Just as you both work towards the wedding, continue to work on the marriage; let your marriage be a planned activity and not a coincidence.

Next to your relationship with God is your relationship with your spouse. It is the most important one on earth. May it ever be so. Let nothing come between you and your spouse. What God has put together, let no person put asunder. Don't put it asunder yourself either.

7. Understanding the Sexual Urge

Research has shown that men have more of a physical need for sex once they are married than women do. Pressure builds up in their glands and causes them to think about sex. God made men to physically need sex. This, however, is not an excuse for a man's lack of self-control. You are not an animal like a dog but are God's creation, made in his image and likeness. Therefore, sex should be understood by the couple. Share feelings and express them appropriately.

For unmarried men, occupy your mind with building your relationship with God first. He will help take your mind off those thoughts of sex. However, for the married man, there are times when your wife cannot engage in sexual intercourse. In such a circumstance, you should control yourself and just enjoy the presence and intimacy of your wife. The pressure will eventually decrease. Relax your mind and just enjoy the presence of sharing your bed together. Marriage is not only about sex. Women have no physical need for sex at certain times in the month. Their hormonal state may cause them to be more interested in sex at other times. I suggest you understand your wife and enjoy each other's company.

Women have an emotional need to be loved and cherished, so we hear, "Men give love to get sex, whereas women give sex to get love." Please don't start an argument over this statement, but let it help you to enjoy your sex life in your marriage. With such information, you should not be quarrelling on meeting sexual needs. A man needs to understand that his wife is not a sex machine or an object, so he should not treat her as such no matter how attractive her body may appear.

Treat your wife with respect when it comes to sex. Let her feel loved, and not like a sex object, to find sexual satisfaction.

Men are compared to cooking gas, and the match is seeing a woman's body shape. When men see an attractive woman, they are turned on and ready to go. While seeing a man's body may do nothing for a woman, one cannot say the same for men. The woman is turned on by words, by touch, by kindness, and by caring. She is like a traditional cooking tool. You need to make the fire, add charcoal or wood, warm it up, and then begin to fan it to get it started, but once the fire is going, you have to keep coming back to fan it or else it will go out. It takes time to get hot, and when it is hot, it is really hot. Such is the case with women. The loving husband will find that his love keeps the wood or charcoal warm all the time, so fanning it to make it hot takes less time. First spend quality time with your wife. Do not start by requesting sex; it will come naturally. I am beginning to sound like a sex educator in a class with couples.

To men, not only do women take a lot of time to heat up, but also they have to unbury the coals from the ashes! Preparing for sex is a mental activity for the woman. You send her the right signal, and depending on how she receives the signal, she will react to it or respond to it. She has to make sure everything else is taken care of first before she comes to bed. When she gets to bed, she starts talking—about the day at work, about the kids at school and on the home front, about the family member who called, about your sister who visited, about money, and about dinner. This is a good sign! She is clearing her mind so that she can focus on her husband and enjoy him. Meanwhile, for the man, don't start your own conversation, as that is not the intention. During that period of her talking, you can gently give her a good massage to calm her nerves, or rub her hands against yours, or just wrap your arms around her and listen to her. If she does not object, this is also a good sign.

Laughter brings people closer and raises emotion. If there was something funny in your day, share it with her. If she pours out her concerns or worries, commit those to the Lord for her in prayer. Prayer is also an essential tool. Commit the matter to the Lord for your wife, and let her hear you express your trust in him (with your arms still wrapped around her). Prayer is a powerful force of oneness. Then she will be ready to start seriously thinking about sex! You must see if this works for you, but according to my research, when this atmosphere is created, women seriously begin to think about sex as a tool of relaxation.

To the woman: remember that your husband needs to *see* his wife. This means you have to come to bed looking your best, fresh and ready.

As I mentioned earlier, preparing for sex is a mental activity for the woman. Therefore a man can tell by the way she has dressed, or by her jovial mood in coming to bed, that when she gets into bed, she wants to be noticed and complimented. You have to mean what you say to her with your attention fully on her. I am imagining a scene with no phone calls or with your telephone on silence; these are signs that you are interested. Words spoken at this moment are very important. Notice how the writer of the Song of Solomon talks about what he *sees* in his wife.

If possible, have a scented candle in the room or a dim light—but a reflective one so you can see all her body movements. You must enjoy your wife. Examine her shape and appreciate her. She is your wife; both of you are naked but not ashamed (Genesis 2:25).

Looking at your wife's naked body gives you, her husband, the guilt-free pleasure of touching her. Women, remember that your husband needs to be able to remember the night before when you were wearing your tight jeans as you walked home from work.

Women, fill your husband's mind with thoughts of your body. In this way, he will think of nothing else but you alone. Make yourself attractive to him always, even when you start having children. Do your best to maintain your shape and retain your beauty. Childbearing is not an excuse to lose your body shape.

In Kenya, I experienced that a lot of women, once they had kids, began to neglect their bodies, breastfeeding their kids in public with their breasts on public display for all to see. In fact, woman, your breast still belongs to your husband. Let him put his head on your bosom at night to sleep. Even in church during Sunday service, young women publicly breastfeed their children in full view of the camera. The idea that you have children and you are no longer attractive to your husband is a lie from the pit of hell. Keep your body in shape and enjoy the best of your marriage.

Most important for a husband to know is that a wife will often give in when she knows you aren't looking for sex. If you start being loving and affectionate only when you want sex, it will make her angry and turn her off. Why? Because she feels like you are treating her like a prostitute.

The only difference is that instead of giving her money for sex, you are giving her kisses for sex. Love her also when she can't give you sex or after you have had sex. Don't just have sex, get up, take a shower, and go about your life as if nothing has happened. The woman is not a sex object, I repeat; therefore, treat her with respect and as your equal partner in the relationship. Your sex relationship should be mutual. Again, don't turn away or fall asleep immediately after sex. Have some conversation, talking to each other, before going to sleep.

Always remember to share this sweet experience and the memories of it as often as possible. Many times, my wife still feels shy when I tell her about how beautiful she is. "Don't you see I am fat?" I tell her, "I just love you the way you are." I expected her to become fat; after twenty years, she could not remain the same size. But I always remember the beautiful young woman I fell in love with. That has not changed.

I have changed as well.

Treat your wife with respect when it comes to sex. Let her feel loved, and not like a sex object whose purpose is your sexual satisfaction.

CHAPTER 17

Preparing for a Wedding

As important as this occasion is, I kindly advise you not to allow the preparation to stress you. Actually some couples start having problems when preparing for the wedding because of over expectation, or trying to overdo it, or modelling their wedding after some others they have witnessed in the past. The first thing I see young men and women who are not married reacting to is the high cost of organizing a wedding. They are afraid of the cost involved. What you need to realize is that your wedding day is your best day after the day you were born to this earth. That said, you should not spend your life's fortune on this one day. There is life after that one-day celebration.

You are leaving both your parents to be joined as man and woman for the rest of your lives. You should give it your best attention and care with all moderation observed. To help you in this process, I have decided to include a checklist for each of you to study and follow. You will want to make photocopies for any other person who is involved in helping you plan the day, but be sure to keep this full set of lists for yourself and for your partner. Never forget that it is not the amount of money you spend on a wedding that guarantees its success. Many times it has to do with the planning, but never forget it is your wedding.

In the end, you are responsible and you need to know what is happening, so make sure it is done properly. In many weddings, the couple leave it all to a wedding planner, but never forget that as good as a wedding planner may be, many are motivated by the money they stand to make from it, so they sometimes persuade you to take on unnecessary costs and expenses. This is so they can make more money for themselves, to the detriment of your wedding.

Wedding planners have made marriage more expensive, but if you can afford them, you should work with them to organize a good wedding for you. In my experience, my spiritual kids, whose weddings I helped plan, kept their wedding costs to a minimum, and they all had wonderful wedding ceremonies with different amounts of money spent according to what they could afford.

Most of us have limited financial resources at our disposal, yet still we can have a once-in-a-lifetime wedding experience. The things that are essential are actually quite small; these can be as expensive or as inexpensive as you want them to be. Most of the expenses will come with the things that you or your family want and not what is necessarily needed for the wedding. It is advisable not to ask your friends to pay for the things on your list! Accept their offers of help, but realize that God's presence is the most important thing you need. You will not want to hear after your wedding a friend or friends boasting that if not for them, you would not have been able to wed. I encountered a couple who nearly suffered a heart attack and a nervous breakdown because they depended on friends who had promised to foot the bill, or who had said that they would pay for the wedding gown or tuxedo, but then those friends disappointed them with the dress never arriving or coming late, sometimes as late as the wedding day itself. For some, they had to make use of an alternative dress for the wedding.

The Wedding

Avoid comments such as "Mr A did his wedding this way, and they had a good wedding show" or "Mr B also had a good wedding show," so then you don't think it is compulsory for you also to have a wedding show like that. I want to say it clearly here, you don't need to put on a wedding show. That is not important at all!

Do not grieve the Holy Spirit because of the sin of greed or covetousness, à la "Mr A did his wedding show in this manner, so mine is going to beat it." A wedding is not a competition. Make time to read the following scriptures: Colossians 3:5; 1 Thessalonians 4:10–12; and 1 Timothy 6:6–10. In your prayer, ask God to help you think of creative alternatives, but not for how to spend money you don't have or money you need to keep to start your life together with your new spouse. Can you imagine that you may use something you already have for your wedding and yet nobody will notice it?

Where have you read in the Bible that you need to buy all things new to use for your wedding? The honest truth is that few will know if an item is new or not. Also, I do not advise that you go borrowing from friends for your wedding, only later to hear that it's been made public that you borrowed. "If not for the fact that I had lent him my suit, he would not have had a successful wedding with her." People often ask me the question "May I borrow from a close friend?" I would prefer that friend bless you rather than your borrowing from them. Just make use of what you have, please.

Most expenses will come from the things that you or your family want and not from what is needed for the wedding.

How you can simplify and yet make your wedding day special?

These checklists will help you plan and work ahead. Some things can only be done in the last few days, but everything else should be taken care of as soon as possible. Free your mind of those issues so that you can concentrate on the big day. Don't leave what you can do now to the end. If there is something you can do today, then do it today!

Please note that you don't have to have everything on the checklists. Each checklist is like a menu; you don't have to order all the meals on the menu, just what you can eat. For example, my wife and I did not make use of bridesmaids and groomsmen, so we didn't need to bother ourselves with clothes for groomsmen and bridesmaids. We only had the maid of honour and the best man, and one little bride and groom, and we had one of the most beautiful weddings I have witnessed, simple as well as classic. On the wedding team were six of us. My brother-in-law walked my wife down the aisle and presented her to me, with five other persons at the altar with us. Now, more than twenty years later, we still enjoy watching our wedding video and looking at the pictures. Our ceremony and reception was simple and beautiful, straight to the point. You can also allow your bridesmaids and groomsmen to wear something from their own collections, such as a nice dress or suit they have in their wardrobe. Just have them choose a similar colour that is in line with your theme for your wedding. My wife gave away her wedding gown some years after we were married to a niece of mine. My niece had a good wedding with the gown, and nobody knew the source of the gown. I was told that many women keep their wedding gowns because they want to fit in them again. The choice is all yours, but don't keep the gown to be buried in it. Ridiculous. Why would you want to be buried in your wedding gown? There is no wedding in heaven for which you will require the gown again. In heaven, we are entering a new marriage where we don't need a gown or a suit. Christ will prepare for you a better angelic gown without stain in heaven. And for many women, after few years, they can no longer fit into their wedding gowns. Why not use the gown, then, to bless someone else who probably cannot afford to spend a lot of money on a new gown? I am not asking you to sell it, but I am suggesting that you use it to bless someone else.

A video recording is nice but not necessary. Very few of the items in the checklists are required, based on my experience and findings while discussing marriage with newly wedded couples. There are a lot of possibilities, such as a combination of video and photographs in one package; you don't need to hire different people for this form of coverage. With modern telephones, you can actually have your wedding recorded and edited to your taste.

- Photo coverage—how many cameramen?
- Newspaper/magazine publication of the wedding announcement
- Gifts to both parents for giving during the wedding
- Use of a musician or DJ to provide music

Cross off what you aren't going to have, unless it has a star beside it and therefore it is important to the wedding preparation.

I want you to remember the purpose of your wedding day as you plan your list—to get married in the presence of God, family, and other witnesses. No matter what else happens or doesn't happen, if you end the day as husband and wife, then your wedding will be a success and you will have started on a rightful path in a martial journey through life.

Again, commit all the planning in prayer to God, and trust your wedding team in your decision-making. Be open to them. Let them know what you want and how you want it, so notes can be compared and the final decision made by you and your partner.

Permission to Wed

After you have talked with your pastor, undergone your marital counselling, and gotten the blessings of both families, it is expected that the church will agree with you on your wedding plans, including the dates and the specifications for the wedding ceremony. It is expected that the church will support you with a wedding team leader to help organize the ceremony. The pastor has a significant role to play in the process and in the execution of the whole wedding plan—putting on the final touches to the arrangement, meeting with both families, talking the couple through the wedding ceremony, and assisting the team through the whole ceremony. The reception plan is mostly the responsibility of the couple now. Where do they intend to have it? Is it going to be part of the church ceremony? Will the reception follow immediately after the wedding ceremony, or will you have a hall reserved for that purpose with the guests moving to that venue after the church wedding?

Is a Church Wedding Really Necessary?

Persons who already are living together as husband and wife before marrying have put this question to me severally: Is it necessary to have a wedding ceremony? I say yes if you are a Christian. It is evidence of your faith in Christ. And if you are not a Christian, would you not like your marriage to be blessed of God, knowing from what you have read that marriage is God's institution? Does this annul all other forms of weddings in existence? No. You can still wed in accordance to your traditional values or your culture, as long as you do not practise those things that are against the Word of God, such as having sex before wedding or having children before wedding.

Let your marriage values be not based on traditional values but on God's values for marriage, which *Getting to Know You* has dealt with in previous chapters. It is also important that you marry before the law of the land or the country where you reside. This helps to legitimize and legalize your marriage before the law, and that entitles you to all necessary benefits as you begin to expand your marriage as husband and wife. If your wedding is not recognized and registered before the law, then your church wedding is not valid before the law and you will be disobeying the law of the land, which itself is a sin against God's Word. Therefore, it is ideal to wed first before the law, followed by the church solemnization. Give to Caesar what belongs to Caesar and to God what belongs to God. There is no confusion in this order.

First Checklist

Date of the wedding	
Wedding venue	
Reception venue	
Officiating minister/pastor	
Contact person's name and telephone number	

Second Checklist

Section A—Bridegroom

Full name as on your passport
Address
Condition before wedding (single/separated/divorced/widower)
Occupation
Residence at the time of wedding
Father's name
Father's occupation

Other Information

Name of best man
Telephone

Section B— Bride

Full name as on your passport
Address
Condition before wedding (single/separated/divorced/widow)
Occupation
Residence at the time of wedding
Father's name
Father's occupation

Other Information

Name of maid of honour
Telephone

It is the responsibility of the officiating pastor to request a letter of approval from the bride's parents. In many cases, the agreement is given verbally, which is OK, but for proper documentation and for your church record, the pastor will want to have this letter as a confirmation that the parents or guardians of the bride have released her for marriage and that she has their blessing to be given in marriage. On the day of the ceremony itself, it is expected that the bride's parents properly hand over their daughter to be given away in marriage.

Letter from the Bride's Parent

Consent of the Bride's Parent

I, Mr _____, being the official parent/guardian of the bride as her (father/ stepfather/uncle/brother), hereby give my consent for our daughter,

Miss _____, to be wedded to Mr _____ in holy matrimony, which will be conducted at the location and date stated.

Signature: _____

Date: _____

Again, in Kenya and probably in some other countries, you need to place a public advertisement three months before the wedding in a local newspaper or on the city council's public notice board of your intention to be wedded to so-and-so and asking if there is any public objection to the proposal.

This is a sample of such an announcement as published in Kenya:

In the matter of the African Christian Marriage and Divorce Act and in the matter of intended marriage, we wish to announce the wedding of _____ [bachelor/widower], son of [father's name] and [mother's name] of the province of _____.

County:
Division:
Location:
Sub-location:
Village:

and

_____ [spinster/widow], daughter of [father's name] and [mother's name], of the province of _____.
County:
Division:
Location:
Sub-location:
Village:

Venue _____

Date _____

Anyone having any objection to the wedding, you must bring such objection(s) before the date given for the wedding.

This notice is actually on display in the public gallery at the provincial district commissioner's office three months prior to the wedding, and if any person has reason to object to the wedding, he or she may put it in writing. Then the government is authorized to investigate the alleged reason or reasons, and the whole wedding arrangement may be suspended or cancelled depending on the truthfulness of the allegation. With such a development, it is not right to continue with the church wedding until you have resolved whatever differences have arisen in the matter.

(This announcement is meant for public reaction; if there is no reaction within that three-month period, then nothing should stand in the way of both the civic and Christian wedding taking place. You can go ahead with all your arrangements.)

Just as the Bible says, "What the Lord has put together, let no man put asunder." Once the given period has expired, the church is given the go-ahead to officiate the wedding ceremony. Failure to follow this procedure as laid out is a violation of the law which is punishable by law. This is an example from Kenya. Every other country has its laws on marriage, and you are expected to know these laws before setting a date for the wedding ceremony.

The same procedure is expected to be followed in the church, at least three to four Sundays on a monthly basis. The announcement of the proposed wedding should be made to the congregation, who are charged with these words: "If you know of any reason why these two persons [names mentioned] should not be joined together in Holy Matrimony, speak now or forever keep your peace." If, after the three or four readings, there is no reaction from the church, it is an approval; there is no man or woman standing against the wedding taking place. The pastor will publicly announce the wedding date before the congregation and pray for the date. Invitation is then opened to all members of the church to attend the wedding. The congregation is to be witnesses on the wedding day.

First Reading

Date: _____

Title/name of the person in charge: _____

Place: _____

Signed: _____

Second Reading

Date: _____

Title/name of the person in charge: _____

Place: _____

Signed: _____

Third Reading

Date: _____

Title/name of the person in charge: _____

Place: _____

Signed: _____

After the four-week announcement period has ended, the two are allowed to sit together in church in preparation for D-Day. They are introduced and announced to the church at every given opportunity to invite witnesses to their wedding. If the intention is not to have a huge wedding feast, the couple may invite guests to their wedding with invitation cards. The documents approving the marriage should be officially stamped, and proof of payment of fees should be provided if fees are involved.

Wedding Checklist

| Groom, bride, wedding coordinator |
| Pastor |
| Venue |
| Date |

Some checklists include not only things to wear, eat, or drink for the event but also your total attitude towards the wedding arrangement.

Check out these lists and tell your partner what you think about them:

Attitude Checklist

- I am not comparing myself with others (2 Corinthians 10:12).
- I am not giving into greed, which is idolatry (Colossians 3:5).
- I am "bearing my own burdens", and I am grateful if others help (Galatians 6:5; Ephesians 5:20).
- I am choosing a heart of contentment in whatever God provides for us (Philippians 4:11).
- I am praying to God to be glorified in our wedding and in our life as we plan it together (1 Corinthians 10:31).

- I am keeping my priorities in focus (Romans 13:8).
- I am keeping my body pure, to be given to my spouse on our wedding night (1 Thessalonians 4:3).

Dowry Checklist

This list is probably not applicable everywhere, but for those readers from Africa, dowry is part of the wedding plan. This is an issue which needs to have long been settled. In some cultures, it is a whole ceremony. For instance, in Kenya, sometimes the pastor is asked to accompany the bridegroom in the dowry presentation to the family of the bride. When the dowry is accepted, there is a ceremony along with it. In some cultures, a provision of cows, goats, sheep, food items, clothes, and money is accepted as dowry. Many times a list is given to the groom ahead of time of the demands of the family of his bride-to-be, and he prepares it. Then a date is fixed for the delivery, at which point he will be accompanied by his family to request the hand of the woman in marriage.

Initial Meeting with Parents

Date:
Accompanied by:
Results:

Second Meeting with Parents

Date:
Accompanied by:
Results:
Date: _____

☐ Agreement reached and permission form filled out.

☐ Permission from the venue (where the wedding will take place).

☐ Forms received and turned in, and of course payment made.

Pastor's Permission

I hereby agree to the wedding of _____ (groom) and _____ (bride) on the date _____ at _____ (venue).

Name of pastor: _____

Date: _____

Signature: _____

Telephone: _____

Invitation Cards

Do not order invitation cards before the pastor's permission has been given and the venue has been settled. This will be viewed as manipulation and may result in permission not being granted for the wedding. Follow the simple procedure; don't act far ahead of your pastor and the wedding committee on the whole plan.

Let your pastor lead you through what the wedding process will entail, such as the seating arrangement and order of service.

God has the right person and the right way to do things. And the right time too! Submit to him and those over you in the Lord. You will be glad you did (see Hebrews 13:17).

Cross-check the list of persons needed for the wedding.

Person responsible for organizing the wedding: _____

Number of persons needed by the groom: _____

Number of persons needed by the bride: _____

Total =

When will the invitation be handed off to the printer? _____

Date of collection of invitation cards from the printer: _____

Paid for _____ (date)

Mailing _____ (person in charge)

Now dates are very important. Indicate the date and time for each activity being organized for the wedding. Set apart time for meetings, and ensure that you are present at those meetings so that nothing is decided for you or in your absence that would spoil the best day of your life.

Both of you getting married must ensure that you attend all meetings. Express whatever you do not agree with during those meetings, and do not try to change things after the team working on your behalf. This could discourage them, and then they will not put their best into your wedding.

The two to be married must always take the last look at the arrangements to be certain that all is according to plan.

Note: For my European readers, using Holland as an example, the marriage arrangement is a bit different. When the two partners finally get engaged and have informed their pastor, they need to inform the municipal council (Gementee) of their intention to get married. This is the process you need to following in the Netherlands. The city council conduct the marriage counselling and agree on a set day for the wedding. They also provide the officials for the wedding. This process is always very short, and a limited number of close relatives and a few friends may be invited. After the ceremony, you are given a wedding certificate or booklet, which you can now present to your church pastor so as to go ahead with the church wedding.

How to Be Wedded by Civil Law in the Netherlands

First you need to notify the municipality. This was previously called a "notice of intent to marry" (*in ondertrouw gaan*). You may announce your intention in any municipality in the Netherlands. It is most practical to do this in the municipality where you will be getting married or where you live.

Many people will probably think, *Why a civil wedding in Holland?* Well, it is required that you have a civil wedding in order to enjoy your marriage benefits as you have the option of living together as well in the Netherlands. Also it is the only valid form of marriage (religious weddings are not legally recognized in Holland), so it is considered as an important event with the spouses expected to energetically participate in the configuration of the ceremony. In fact you are not allowed to have any form of religious wedding before the civil wedding is done. Many have ignored this warning, but if you are caught doing so, you pay a heavy fine/penalty. Just keep your positive spirit, and you can have the wedding ceremony of your dreams instead of a typical common civil marriage.

For this civil wedding ceremony to take place, the municipal council requires some things from both persons, such as the following (you must have a resident permit that enables you to live in the country, or else you cannot marry. If you are in the process of obtaining such a permit, all necessary documents must be submitted for verification and approved before you can go ahead):

- Birth certificate translated to English or Dutch
- Certificate of civil status in English or Dutch (only if one or both of the intended spouses were previously married; otherwise it is not necessary)
- Proof of registration in a Dutch municipality
- Certificate of previous marriage(s) and divorce papers translated to Dutch or English (if one or both of the intended spouses were previously married)
- Copies of identity card or passport
- Copies of the identity cards or the passports of people you choose as witnesses, at least two persons

Important Note: However, since my experiences from the Dutch and Nigeria public sectors have not been exactly positive, I recommend that you ask the employees of the municipality what is absolutely necessary and what is not necessary to get married in order to avoid transferring certificates from wherever you came from to the Netherlands and vice versa. Allow me to take a few moments to outline what you should know in general for a civil marriage in the Netherlands:

You need to make an appointment with a municipality. In the past you could walk in and get a date for your appointment, but now the dates are usually booked through the online appointment. You just fill out a digital form on the municipality's website, choosing which town hall you want to go, on what date, and at what time. Attention: Be sure that you start the whole procedure in the town hall you want to get married in and not a different one; otherwise, it is possible that you will get married in a town hall you don't want, or you will lose a lot of time waiting for your papers to be transferred from one town hall to another (and trust me, this could take some time!).

In the Netherlands you may get married if your age is eighteen years old or older, if you are not married currently, and if you are permanent citizen of the country (or you have a residence permit). If these conditions are met, then you are allowed to request for this civil marriage ceremony within the country.

If your marriage is not recognized and registered before the law, your church marriage will not be valid before the law and you will be disobeying the law of the land, which itself is a sin against God's Word.

You should have at least two witnesses, but not more than four, and each should be eighteen years old or older. At least fifteen days before the wedding ceremony, you and your partner must sign a prewedding agreement in which you both state your intention to get marry. The day that you sign this agreement, you have the right to take a day off from your job (this is an extra day off in addition to your annual vacation days). And of course you'll take another day off—the day you get married (if you get married on a weekday). Remember that you have to wait at least fifteen days in order to get married for good. During those fifteen days, intended spouses have the chance to cancel their marriage if they regret their decision. (As you see, Dutch law takes care of everything!)

There is a variety of places where you can get married. Most people get married in a town hall, but this is not necessary for your own marriage! Employees of a municipality will provide you with a list of different places inside and outside the city where you live so you can choose the ideal place for your wedding. My wife and I chose the simplicity of the city hall in Amsterdam (it was really simple and moderate, accommodating at least twenty persons).

You will realize quickly that the total cost you will need to pay for a town hall varies depending on the day, the hour, and the place where you will decide to have your wedding ceremony. In the schedule provided, you will see that there are days and hours of the week when you can get married for free or at little cost, while there are other days (basically weekends) for which, if you pick them, you will have to pay more—even up to fifteen hundred euros! If you have not received a call from the town hall regarding your wedding ceremony, don't hesitate to call them and complain that they forgot you.

A few days before the wedding, an organizer (who will be probably the master of ceremonies too) will call you to discuss in detail the wedding process. He or she will ask you dozens of things, such as if you wish to have the ceremony in Dutch or in English. Moreover, the organizer will ask you for personal details from your life and your partner's life too (how you met each other, how your relationship has been until now, how you decided to get married, how you proposed to the other, etc.). You will need to decide if you and your partner will exchange vows, if you will exchange rings, or if someone among the guests will speak for you.

On the big day, try to be at least half an hour early in getting to the town hall. A wedding ceremony always starts on time, and it lasts no more than thirty minutes. The master of ceremonies, based on what you have discussed with him or her beforehand, will give you a wedding ceremony close to what you have dreamed of. He or she will read a personal story about you and your partner, will ask both of you to read your vows, and will ask you to exchange rings (if this is what you have decided). Then you and your partner will sign the wedding papers, and afterwards the master of ceremonies will call the witnesses to sign the wedding document as witnesses. The ceremony will end after the master of ceremonies communicates his or her best wishes to the newlyweds. A marriage certificate is received after the ceremony. The master of ceremonies congratulates the couple first, and after that all the other guests give their congratulations. The newly wedded couple departs with their guests to whatever other arrangements they have made. That is how it goes with the municipal wedding, but it is compulsory to have this ceremony done before your church wedding can take place.

CHAPTER 18

Tips for the Newly Wedded

A famous songwriter, Joe Thomas, wrote this in one of his popular songs, "I Wanna Know", "I'd like to know what makes you cry so I can always be the one who makes you smile."

I find this song to express the whole essence of marriage; it is about how to treat each other better. I know the woman feels she deserves to be treated nicer, but I say that the man and the woman both deserve to be treated nice in the marriage—and it starts from day one.

Remember all the love you expressed on that first day, looking into each other's eyes and declaring, "I love you. And yes, I do" Let it not be a once-per-year remembrance. I see everyone going crazy about one day called Valentine's Day, which some people call Lovers' Day. Every day should be Lovers' Day in your marriage. After the wedding, the marriage itself, the process of living together as one, begins. It is never the easiest thing to do, but you can make it as easy as possible.

As a gentleman, you will agree with me that a man who is well cultured, educated, sensitive, and well mannered in society is expected to have these same qualities displayed and applied in his marriage as he builds his relationship with his spouse. A gentleman is exactly what the name suggests: a man who is gentle. A man should take care of his wife and treat her with the utmost respect because he knows very well that it is because of a woman that he exists in the first place.

Every woman wants to secure for herself one of these rare species—a gentle man. So what does every woman want from her own gentleman? Below is what you will find in every woman's "My Ideal Man" list. Maybe it's worded differently, but it's the same altogether: This list is not comprehensive, but if a man takes this to heart, he will find his wife to be more enjoyable and his marriage to be sweeter than honey.

Try it out.

These tips work both ways. As much as they are for the woman, the man expects that as he provides these things for his wife, the wife will be kind enough to reciprocate the love and gesture in the same manner.

Be Respectful

A respectful man understands his wife's worth. You married her, so it is time to assign to her that worth, not once but always in the marriage. You will have to give her what she needs and deserves, and you will have to appreciate her always. You will need to be sensitive to her feelings. Once these things are done, I assure you, you will get the best out of your wife and make her the best in the whole wide world. You will write to me in a few months to tell me, "Your tips are working." And if you are not able to meet any of her requests or demands, explain to her politely and not with violence, not ignoring her as if she does not exist. Treat her with the utmost respect; always remember, she is your helper and partner in the marriage and not a lower being or weaker being.

Be Loyal

Just the way a man will be loyal to his God, so he is expected to be loyal to his wife. How are you expected to be loyal to your God? It is time to read your Bible again. Make it a companion in your marriage, and read it along with your wife. In the Bible are enough examples of loyalty towards God. In the first place, God is loyal to his people, protecting and providing for us. I know that for those of us who are football fans or tennis fans, we are loyal to the team we support and loyal to the players. A wife craves for a man who will be loyal to her. How a woman recognize such a man is by comparing him to the one she is married to. A man whose eyes don't wander from woman to woman is loyal to his wife no matter what happens. Men, you have to show your loyalty; it is not just words alone, and it is not a one-time thing. It is something that you must always do in the marriage. Defend your wife, love her, brag about her, talk about her, treat her right, etc. I remember in my first year in Kenya, I was told that I talked too much about my wife in the church and that some men in the congregation felt threatened, particularly Luo men, who are not used to talking about their wives in the public. All of that changed. Once I'd taught them the right things to say and do to their wives, their marriages were strengthened. I taught them the value of being loyal to their wives, saying that they get the best out of their wives when their wives trust in their loyalty towards them.

Be Attentive

Attentiveness will always improve the communication, and eventually the bond, of two people. I cannot emphasize this enough for a marriage. Women are more attentive, research has shown, so a wife expects an attentive husband too. Wives are attention seekers. If you make your wife feel like she doesn't have to fight for your attention because you constantly give it to her, then you've found yourself a lifelong companion, and you are going to enjoy a healthy marriage. In addition to being attentive, you must also learn to be a good listener. Wives always have much to say about everything, and if you start having children, you must be prepared to pay more attention to your wife. A wife does not want to share her personal attention with the children. Men struggle with this as children begin to demand the attention of their dad as well, through either sports or other activities. It would be advisable that you do things together as a family so that no competition arises for your attention.

Be Responsible

Knowing what your role is in the marriage helps reduce stress for your wife. The worst experience is when roles are shifted by the man or abandoned to the wife. I hear some women say, "I am like the husband in this house. I take all the initiative, and even some important decisions are left to me." The type of man this describes is going to have trouble with his marriage. A wife wants her husband to be the leader in the house. The man who makes decisions for his family through responsible actions is ever loved. A man who plays his role well will encourage his wife to play her part just as well and even beyond expectations. A wife shouldn't have to feel as if she is responsible for two people or more people just because her man is not playing his part.

Be a Defender

God is our ultimate defender and our shield, but as a man, you are God's representative in your family. And as I mentioned earlier, your wife demands attention and even more from her husband.

One of the ways you give her attention is to let her know that you are there to defend her. She is not expecting you to engage in a fight on her behalf, but she needs to know that you as her man are there always as someone to rely on and depend upon in times of trouble, for ideas, knowledge, and wisdom on certain subjects in the marriage. What your wife will not forgive you for is if you chicken out on her when she needs you most. Therefore, there is nothing that will show your love for your wife better than defending her and her love for you. Defending her love assures her that you love her and that your marriage is for life.

Be the bigger person and apologize after a bad argument. And don't let matters get out of hand, leading you to become a wife beater or abuser. Your good conduct will cause your wife to love you more!

Be Ambitious

There's nothing as sexy as an ambitious husband. A man with ambition in a marriage is the darling of the wife. A woman will go to any lengths to satisfy such a man. The wife wants to know how far her husband is willing to go to take care of her, even when she earns more income than he. You should understand that it is not about the money you make that satisfies the woman, but the limit to which you are willing to go to show your love for her. A woman wants a man who comes up with motivational ideas, either for his own personal growth or for that of his wife. Many women love to be challenged in their marriage to be better than when they entered into it. Let it not be through insults or through comparison to other people. Ambition with proper encouragement will bring out the best in the marriage. Ambition just goes to show how much a husband is willing to take care of his wife and do other things, keeping them in check to make life easier for both spouses and for the rest of the family. The ambition rubs off. In this, a husband makes his wife want to be a better person.

Be Trustworthy

Many of my points I am making in this chapter are taken from my understanding of the respective biblical principle. A trustworthy man is a man into whose hands every woman wants to lay her life. In fact, there is a shortage of words to express the type of confidence a woman has in such a man. A man you can trust is a man you want to keep in your life forever. I mean, a wife who has a trustworthy husband doesn't have to worry about many things such as sexually transmitted diseases, or whether he is part of a gang, or if he is a wanted man, a criminal, or a gambler—or all of these negative things. The strongest key to keeping your marriage healthy is to build it on trust, absolute trust as Jesus Christ taught us in the Bible, as he trusted the Father with his life to the very end. Wives already have so many things on their minds to worry about, but the last worry they want to have is lack of trust in their husbands. Once a wife comes to distrust her husband, the marriage is bound to hit the rocks or crash. The reason for the increase in divorce cases today is basically that one of the partners is no longer trustworthy. That the other person is not faithful is not an excuse for you to become unfaithful. You must stay faithful and trustworthy. You're probably asking, *What will my reward be for remaining faithful and trustworthy?* Well, just remember that good deeds attract reciprocation. Let husbands do to their wives what they expect them to do to them. If you follow this advice, you will see that your marriage will be one admired by others, something they wish to emulate.

This is a short story of two of my trusted spiritual children in Kenya. I am very proud of them. I share their testimonies in *Getting to Know You* for your encouragement. Carolyne is a beautiful nursing sister. Her husband-to-be at the time was a young medical doctor, fresh from university, with a promising career ahead of him. They were both members of our church in Kisumu, Kenya. When I met them, they were about to break up their relationship because they were both experiencing stress, given the nature of their jobs, and they weren't sure they were meant for each other. During my conversation with them, I asked them how well they knew each other. That probably sounds like a strange question for two people who claim to be in love.

Here is Carolyne's account of how she came to meet the love of her life:

> In January 2009, I was a student nurse on attachment at Provincial General Hospital in Nyanza, where I was working in the theatre as a scrub nurse for any surgeon carrying out an operation.
> There was the surgeon and Dr Kevin Omamo Ndai, who was then the surgeon's assistant. This is how I first met him: I remember the surgeon requested that Kevin escort me back to my college hostel because the operation had taken longer than expected and it was a bit late, around 8.30 p.m. He refused, saying that he hadn't come all that way to work just to escort a woman back to her college hostel. So I left on my own. He and I did not see each for a long time after that episode, despite the fact that we worked at the same hospital. I was subsequently moved

to another ward. One night we bumped into each other when I was wheeling a patient from the theatre back to the ward after an operation. This time he tried to speak to me, asking where I had been and saying that he was wondering where I had disappeared to. I did not give him any attention, of course.

Months later we became friends, and before I knew what was happening, in April 2010, he proposed marriage to me. For sure I said yes. That is how we came to be where we are today. As you can imagine, I have left out the romantic part of the story, but you understand.

On the side, Dr Kevin Omamo, he reflected on the relationship. Years later, he began to appreciate what he would have missed if he had not gotten to know Carolyne better.

I first met Carolyne as a sister in the church. She was visiting us as a student nurse. During my chat with her, she told me about her relationship with Dr Omamo. She wasn't really sure if she wanted a relationship. According to her, he was too busy to have time for her. I encouraged her to invite Dr Kevin Omamo to visit the church, so we could get together and talk. He came. In fact, he loved the church and the preaching. He then committed himself to our church. After that, I could talk to him more often about his relationship with Carolyne.

They came to me one time to tell me that they wanted to end the relationship; they still hadn't been able to put it together. I asked them to agree to undergo some counselling sessions as they were having some personality challenges. Basically, it was a challenge of getting to know each other better because of the nature of their work. They seemed not to have enough time for themselves. I advised them on certain things to do, and I gave them separate assignments based on their relationship. After two weeks, I asked them how it was going, but Carolyne told me that she still wanted to end the relationship. I asked her again why, but she didn't have an answer for me. I came to the conclusion that they needed some breathing space and they needed to take the relationship more seriously with God. Pray for it, work for it, and trust God for it. I advised both of them to minimize their coming together for a period of time, and separately pray about their relationship. "Be open to one another with regard to whatever God reveals to you about the relationship; be honest enough to tell the other person if you truly love him or her, and be willing to work on your differences," I said. They did as I'd requested, and I am sure they did it diligently. After one week of prayer and fasting, they both came back to me to express their interest in continuing with their relationship, also saying that they were willing to be helped to walk through all they needed to learn about marriage before they said yes to one another.

Once they became open to each other and began talking about everything, the relationship blossomed beyond imagination. They began to show a commitment to the things of God. Carolyne was in the Praise and Worship team of our church, and Kevin had joined the Bible study group. He led Bible studies, led intercession, and helped with church administration despite his job. They were both happy in working for the Lord. I wasn't surprised. After they had consulted with their respective families, they consulted with me. After that, they officially announced their engagement, and we began preparing for the wedding in earnest. The wedding took place at the sports ground of Tom Mboya Labour College in Kisumu, Kenya, on 19 March 2011. They are blessed with two children, and they still love their lives together as husband and wife, Dr and Mrs Kevin Omamo Ndai. Dr Ndai post this to his Facebook account on the occasion of his wedding anniversary: "Who so findeth a wife findeth a good thing, and obtaineth favour of the Lord' (Proverbs 18:22). Lord, thanks for the favour I received when I found Her Excellency, the Most Adorable, Queen of Omamo Ndai Heart Island, Carolyne Adienge." Dr Kevin Omamo is enjoying his marriage. I have visited them after a few years, and they are still in love.

Dr Omamo is not even ashamed to share it with thousands of Facebook fans; he is still appreciative of the wife God gave him. But it was not always like that in the past. The same Dr Omamo wrote this in a separate message of appreciation for his wife on the occasion of her birthday: "Four years ago at the now Jaramogi Oginga Odinga Teaching and Referral Hospital, I was obnoxiously rude, unfair, and indifferent to the most beautiful woman I had ever seen. Little did I know that she would be the love of my life, my best friend, and the mother of my children, Jalaam and Joy. My dearest Carolyne Adienge, happy birthday!"

I am sure that the story of Carolyne and Dr Kevin Omamo will inspire any person who wants a serious relationship but is presently having challenges in this area. You need someone to talk to, and you need to give yourself a break and to focus on God for direction. Get to know the person from the eyes of God; you will not see the shortcomings but the gifting from God.

Kevin and Carolyne are just two of the several young men and women God has used my wife and me to inspire and to bless their wedding in Kenya. Today I am still part of their lives as I continue to enjoy witnessing the glory of God in their lives.

CHAPTER 19

How to Have a Good Marriage

The man said, "This is now bone of my bones and flesh of my flesh; she shall be called 'woman', for she was taken out of man." For this reason a man will leave his father and mother and be united to his wife, and they will become one flesh.

—Genesis 2:23–24

A Balanced Look

God sees the marriage as two becoming one. Humankind should see marriage as the process of becoming one. Marriage means embarking upon a journey towards a new way of life. Marriage is a picture of the two of you together in Christ. Just as you are united in the spirit with your Lord's Spirit, so in the flesh you are united with your spouse through marriage. Marriage is a picture of salvation and the resulting growth that occurs thereafter. We experience conflicts in our every step towards spiritual maturity, along with growth in life, and it is no different for the married life. Therefore, you need to see marriage in its proper perspective and find a balance. Imbalance will always result in conflict. Where there is imbalance (conflict) in the marriage, there is spiritual conflict (imbalance) as well. How do you resolve this? Through God and with the help of the wise counsellors around the two of you. You must realize that conflict is a warning signal that something is wrong, and you need to find out what it is and fix it. It starts like a crack on the wall. It usually starts small, and if you don't do anything about it, it becomes bigger with each passing day. When there is a crack, many times it is God's way of trying to get your attention so that he can spiritually reveal to you a troubled spot in your life. The outward conflict always has an inward source. Seek to come to an understanding of what that outward conflict is by seeking the Lord inwardly. The way you do this is through prayer. There is a stronghold that the Lord desires to bring to the surface. The Lord is trying to reveal to you his truth. Ask for it, seek it, and knock for it, and it will be revealed to you.

Probably the most read portion of scripture concerning marriage and its roles is Ephesians

5:21–6:4. It is also the most misunderstood scripture. There is a balance that is often not considered.

Husband and Wife Are Equal in a Marriage

All of us were created before God as equal. You will stand before him as an equal. Yet, just as the whole body of Christ is equal, each of us has different gifts and talents and different roles to fulfil. These are roles the Lord has called you to. One of these is the role of being accountable to your family. The man is the family shepherd; the wife is his helpmate; and the children are his flock, whom both husband and wife are to nurture, love, care for, and train. This picture does not make the man or woman a superior partner but, rather, an equal partner in the task given to them in marriage.

The husband has absolutely no right to dictatorship, tyranny, or abuse in the marriage simply because he has the role of the shepherd. Just as the shepherd of the church, he is not authorized to abuse his office to lead the people. This is not, and never was intended to be, the husband's role. The wife is not a slave, a doormat, or a second-class partner, nor was she ever intended to be so. The husband and wife are to willingly, in love, submit themselves to one another, placing the needs of the other before their own in an unconditional selfless love. This is the true essence of marriage. Marriage is like a ministry, serving one another, meeting each one's needs, and reaching out as an expression of God's love extended towards the other. Nothing less is expected from the man and woman than mutual understanding in all things. In my few years of marriage, I have discovered that my wife's happiness is my happiness, so when I do the unexpected for her, she is overjoyed. I break the usual rules - preparing her nice meal, for instance, before she returns from her job. While she is already thinking on how she is going to cope with her tiredness and with still having to cook for the family, I cook as a surprise, sharing the task with our girls. It is a pleasant surprise for my wife, and we all have dinner together in joy and happiness as one family. It was not a one-time thing but is a practice now in our family. We do it for each other—pleasant surprise—and she loves it.

The wife is to willingly submit herself to meet her husband's needs, and to recognize his role as shepherd, and to support him in that role. This support is to include intercession and understanding.

Basically, it is doing all that is necessary to help her husband be what God intended him to be. I often hear wives complaining about their husbands as not living up to their expectations. What are you doing as a helpmate to make your husband the man you expect him to be? Are you praying for him? Are you talking with him about his doings? Are you in tune with him on his plans? Does your spirit agree with him? Listen, you are one—never forget that—so if your spirit does not agree with his, you may not be in agreement to get the result you desire. Therefore, you need to lock hands together with him to achieve those expectations in your heart of what God is calling him to do.

Be a Good Husband

The obvious advice for any husband, young or old, is to be faithful to your wife. Marriage is the sacred act of two becoming one. That cannot happen, or cannot continue to exist, if another person or interest is brought into the picture. Three or more cannot become one! That is the simple reason I am against every other form of marriage which is not between a man and a woman. If a man is allowed to marry more than one wife, which of the wives is bonded to him as one? It means that he is divided among the wives; the man is incomplete in this context and is not performing his function. In such a circumstance, a man is not able to be completely effective. Proverbs 5:15 reads, "Drink water from your own cistern, running water from your own well. Be faithful to your wife. It is not possible to fetch water from two wells at the same time, you will go from one to another, that is not proper, you have to have your own well and where you can do whatever pleases you at your well."

Ecclesiastes 9:9 reads, "Enjoy life with your wife, whom you love, all the days of this meaningless life that God has given you under the sun, all your meaningless days. For this is your lot in life and in your toilsome labour under the sun."

The scripture is saying that you should enjoy your wife because this life is not that long enough to share yourself with someone else.

Live Joyfully with Your Wife

Do not share your wife with your job, your hobbies, or your television shows. If you travel all week for your job, don't spend your weekend playing golf. Remember, the whole week you are gone, someone is waiting patiently for your return, and she needs you. Both your presence and your touch are important for your wife. This is why she chose you over others, so that you would become hers and hers alone.

> You ask, "Why?" It is because the Lord is acting as the witness between you and the wife of your youth, because you have broken faith with her, though she is your partner, the wife of your marriage covenant. Has not [the Lord] made them one? In flesh and spirit they are his. And why one? Because he was seeking godly offspring. So guard yourself in your spirit, and do not break faith with the wife of your youth. "I hate divorce," says the Lord God of Israel, "and I hate a man's covering himself with violence as well as with his garment," says the Lord Almighty. So guard yourself in your spirit, and do not break faith. (Malachi 2:14–16)

God is saying here in the scriptures that marriage is a covenant. In order to have a job, you entered into agreement with your employer, a form of binding agreement to work faithfully and to be loyal and committed for the course of the job. You did the same when you entered into marriage with your wife, but this time it was even deeper. What happens if you break your agreement with your employer? Do you expect him to praise you? To thank you? To pay you a fat salary? No. So why would you think breaking your marriage covenant is OK? A covenant is sacred and binding! The only thing that can break a covenant is separation by death. In your marriage covenant, God is a witness between you and your spouse. Simply put, God knows! If there is a problem in the marriage, don't you think God, who is the first witness, has the right to know what is going on and to be allowed to apply his wisdom in helping you to solve the problem in your marriage?

The husband absolutely has no right of dictatorship, tyranny, or abuse in the marriage simply because he has the role of shepherd.

CHAPTER 20

Sex in Marriage

I need to write about the subject of sex because in some Christian doctrines, sex is treated as a taboo, only to be applied for childbearing, and never to be talked about. It is just expected to happen naturally. I totally disagree with that notion. Even among animals, there is a sequence of activities for having sex. For human beings, it is a process, and as husband and wife, you are permitted within the context of marriage to enjoy it.

Never listen to the lies which arise from the pit of hell that you are sinning when you have sex with your wife. It is not true. It is a lie. You have a right to sexual pleasure in your marriage. Sexual pleasure is part of your covenant of marriage, sharing your body and the intimacy involved. In marriage, it is lovemaking, not having sex, if I may be permitted to use the proper word. You cannot fulfil your marriage vows by withholding the beauty of lovemaking. The connotation of sex is what makes it look as if it is a sin for a husband to have sexual intercourse with his wife. What you are actually doing is expressing your love for her, which includes satisfaction of her bodily urge and her emotions.

Do not deprive each other except by mutual consent—and then only for a time. As we read in 1 Corinthians 7:3–5, "The husband should fulfill his marital duty to his wife, and likewise the wife to her husband. The wife's body does not belong to her alone but also to her husband. In the same way, the husband's body does not belong to him alone but also to his wife. Do not deprive each other except by mutual consent and for a time, so that you may devote yourselves to prayer. Then come together again so that Satan will not tempt you because of your lack of self-control."

Now I want you to realize that the head of every man is Christ and the head of the woman is man, and the head of Christ is God. (1 Corinthians 11:3)

However, each one of you also must love his wife as he loves himself, and the wife must respect her husband. (Ephesians 5:33)

Husbands, love your wives and do not be harsh with them. (Colossians 3:19)

If anyone does not provide for his relatives, and especially for his immediate family, he has denied the faith and is worse than an unbeliever. (1Timothy 5:8)

Husbands, in the same way be considerate as you live with your wives, and treat them with respect as the weaker partner and as heirs with you of the gracious gift of life, so that nothing will hinder your prayers.

There are more than enough scriptures that point to the fact that man and woman should not deny each other of their body, in that sense it includes all the five senses of sight, smell, taste, touch and hear to fulfill all of these scriptures. (1 Peter 3:7)

For the woman, you are expected to be a good wife. But how do you become a good wife? Following are some points for you on how to be a good wife:

Be a Good Wife

The Lord God said, "It is not good for the man to be alone. I will make a helper suitable for him." Now the Lord God had formed out of the ground all the beasts of the field and all the birds of the air. He brought him or her to the man to see what he would name him or her; and whatever the man called each living creature, that was its name. So the man gave names to all the livestock, the birds of the air and all the beasts of the field. But for Adam no suitable helper was found. So the Lord God caused the man to fall into a deep sleep; and while he was sleeping, he took one of the man's ribs and closed up the place with flesh. Then the Lord God made a woman from the rib he had taken out of the man, and he brought her to the man. The man said, "This is now bone of my bones and flesh of my flesh; she shall be called woman, 'for she was taken out of man'." For this reason a man will leave his father and mother and be united to his wife, and they will become one flesh. (Genesis 2:18–24)

This is the original design of marriage by God. He asked the man and woman to leave their parents behind and unite as one. Too many marriages include the husband's parents, the wife's parents, the siblings of the husband and the wife, and other people. Remember, the two become one—not the four or six become one. Marriage is between a man and his wife and God—no one else! You men, quit running to your mothers every time your wife doesn't do something right in your eyes. The same goes for you wives! Leave your parents out of your marriage, as hard and as tough as this may be for you. If you will not do this, then stay unmarried and live the rest of your life with your parents. I know you don't want that, so if you have made the decision to find a life partner, stay with him through the thick and thin and through the thorns of life.

Wives, in the same way be submissive to your husbands so that, if any of them do not believe the word, they may be won over without words by the behavior of their wives, when they see the purity and reverence of your lives. Your beauty should not come from outward adornment, such as braided hair and the wearing of gold jewelry and fine clothes. Instead, it should be that of your inner self, the unfading beauty of a gentle and quiet spirit, which is of great worth in God's sight. For this is the way the holy women of the past who put their hope in God used to make themselves beautiful. They were submissive to their own husbands, like Sarah, who obeyed Abraham and called him her master. You are her daughter if you do what is right and do not give way to fear. Husbands, in the same way be considerate as you live with your wives, and treat them with respect as the weaker partner and as heirs with you of the gracious gift of life, so that nothing will hinder your prayers. (1 Peter 3:1–7)

This is another one of the most misused scriptures in the Bible. Submission is not slavery! This text does not mean wives are to be ruled by their husbands. Once again, the plan of marriage is for the two to become one. If one is the ruler, then the other person automatically becomes a subject or a slave; they are no longer one. The text in this context means that the man is to be the man. He leads, but his wife walks beside him, not behind him or in front of him. If your wife is behind you, then something is not right. Encourage her to come and walk beside you as a helper. If your wife walks beside you, she can reach out to you when you are in need. Remember, God used Adam's rib to create Eve, not his tail. Walk side by side as husband and wife.

A wife of noble character is her husband's crown, but a disgraceful wife is like decay in his bones.
Be a honourable wife, the one the husband is proud to display for the whole world to see. Show the world your respect for your husband, treat him like your king, have you seen where a queen treats her king with all royalty and majesty. Learn to do this and you will be the crown that fits his head only alone. (Proverbs 12:4)

The wise woman builds her house, but with her own hands the foolish one tears hers down. Wife, you have the power to build your house into a home. Do it with love and patience. It is wisdom that woman applies when your husband acts foolish, people say thrown him away or divorce him but the wise woman learns to forgive, help the husband into full recovery and the husband learn from his foolish acts and does not repeat it again. (Proverbs 14:1)

A foolish son is his father's ruin, and a quarrelsome wife is like a constant dripping. Houses and wealth are inherited from parents, but a prudent wife is from the Lord. (Proverbs 19:13–14)

Can you be a prudent wife? A nagging wife only brings problems to her marriage. Hold your tongue as best as you can, woman. I know it is sharp, but do not use it to cut down your marriage. It is to build your marriage up. Remember, God does not make a mistake when he brings two people together. It is to complement each other. If you are hot, God will give you a man who is as cold as ice. Learn to be cool, especially by following your husband's lead. If he says "enough", then let it be enough and hold your peace.

Again, as we read in 1 Corinthians 7:4–5, "The wife's body does not belong to her alone but also to her husband. In the same way, the husband's body does not belong to him alone but also to his wife. Do not deprive each other except by mutual consent and for a time, so that you may devote yourselves to prayer. Then come together again so that Satan will not tempt you because of your lack of self-control."

Do not hold back your love and affection from your husband. Make yourself as attractive as the day when you first said yes to him. You still can remember your wedding day; your husband said "whaoo" when you came out with your gorgeous gown or dress and beautiful make-up, everything perfect for a groom. But then when you were alone, you showed each other your nakedness, and again it was "whaoo". You were not ashamed, and you didn't go to bed in your wedding gown or tuxedo. Do the same in your marriage now. Make yourself attractive to your husband even as you grow older together in marriage. I see women who cease caring for their bodies as soon as they start having children. Child or no child, stay that beautiful woman your husband married. Period.

Submission is not slavery.

A Threefold Cord

A Christian marriage must be built according to the pattern established by God in the book of Genesis. The first gift you should give each other should be the Bible (the guide to life before leaving the earth). When one is so built on the Word of God, it becomes a pillar in the kingdom of God and his house. A couple who submit their lives to the lordship of Jesus Christ will have supernatural strength in their marriage. Jesus becomes a partner in their marriage, and "a threefold cord is not quickly or easily broken" (Ecclesiastes 4:12).

But it takes some effort on our part to have a successful marriage in this measure. It's not automatic or accidental; we have to work at it. Here are a few specific areas to concentrate on in building your marriage:

1. Focus on the good things about your spouse. Ephesians 5:20–33 makes it clear that God's ideal design for marriage is based on loving your spouse as Christ loves you. You should extend grace to one another as you work to build a godly marriage.
2. Sanctify your home by washing it with the Word of God. Speaking in the context of marriage, the apostle Paul tells us that God's Word has the power to cleanse and make holy (Ephesians 5:25–26). Pray the Word over your spouse and your children. Pray the promises, not the problems, and speak what God says about your mate and your marriage into existence.

3. Husbands, love your wives. God has commanded husbands to love their wives. So if you ask, he will give you his love to give to your wife and will show you ways to demonstrate it to her. Ask him to show you how you can give of yourself to your wife and put her needs above your own. Work on building companionship with your wife, devoting time and effort to communication. Spending time together is critically important to your marriage, and that doesn't mean just watching television together or eating a meal together. Display your affection with words and deeds. Tell your wife you love her as often as possible, even when you are separated for a few hours, days, weeks, or months! Kiss her goodbye when you leave, and give her a nice hug when you come home.

4. Wives, respect your husbands. A wife helps to build a strong marriage by building up her husband. Your ministry is to respect, honour, and encourage your husband. Remember, life and death is in the power of your tongue (Proverbs 18:21). A woman's attitude determines her altitude. Don't be nagging or argumentative with your husband; it is not a good example for you and your children or for other people who may be watching you (Proverbs 27:15). Make your home as warm and wonderful as you can. It's more important to have a home where your husband feels comfortable than to have a showplace. Many men who love to hang out elsewhere after they've married do so simply because their homes or houses are not comfortable. After work, a man should be in a hurry to get home. I love my home and enjoy the comfort it provides. It is relaxing to be with my wife and share the experiences of the day with her.

5. Don't neglect the importance of a fulfilling sexual relationship. Apart from a covenant relationship submitted to God, sex can be selfish in the marriage. But when the Lord is at the centre of a marriage, sex is a part of giving to one another. Scripture tells us that neglecting sexual intimacy opens the door to Satan's attacks (1 Corinthians 7:5). It's your privilege to be God's gift to meet the sexual needs of your spouse. Do your best to be attractive to your spouse and to enjoy each other.

6. Create an atmosphere of romance. In line with point 5, create that atmosphere for both of you to desire each other. Particularly the woman has the power to arouse the interest of her husband to the point that he will never have enough of you and he will not have time to look outside the marriage.

Make yourself attractive to your husband even as you grow older together in marriage.

7. Work together to solve any marital problems. Problems will arise in every marriage. But if you have a good spiritual relationship with the Lord and with each other, you can work through any problem. Magnify your own weaknesses, and minimize those of your spouse. Rather than trying to improve your mate, allow God to deal with you and improve you so you can become a good complement to your husband. If you are willing to die to yourself and let the Lord live through you, he will help you solve every problem that comes your way in your marriage.

8. Strive to make your marriage an excellent one. I do not buy into the argument or discussion that humankind is imperfect, and therefore we give room for mistakes and

faults. I would rather say, let us aspire to excellence in all that we do, including our marriages. You can be excellent in your marriage, and it is not for you to boast but to acknowledge the goodness of God in your marriage.

How to be excellent in all you think or do in your marriage:

1. "Serve wholeheartedly, as if you were serving the Lord, not people, because you know that the Lord will reward each one for whatever good they do, whether they are slave or free" (Ephesians 6:7–8).
2. In your marriage, serve one another with all your hearts as if you were serving God himself. Wives, imagine you serving your husbands as you would serve Jesus Christ when he was on the face of the earth, pouring oil on his head, serving him with all your body, soul, and mind.
3. "Each one should use whatever gift he has received to serve others, faithfully administering God's grace in its various forms" (1 Peter 4:10).
4. Your effectiveness as a Christian is ultimately measured by your ability to demand excellence and get excellence from yourself. How? Through your marriage. In fact, the apostle Paul says that if you can't even love your wife and your children, what business do you have leading God's people? This means that it starts and finishes with you. You have to love your wife and no one else. You have to make your marriage an excellent institution for others to admire and desire to have.
5. Be tough. Don't let the importance of positive reinforcement downplay the need for toughness and discipline in your marriage. It is not a football game where you win some and lose some. It is a win-win situation in marriage, and you have to be determined about that and work towards it too. To do something wrong and not correct the mistake is just another way of showing you don't care about your marriage. Knowing that you believe in excellence and that you won't accept anything less is what inspires most people. So should your marriage be in the eyes of observers, causing them to want the same type of marriage.
6. Spotlight one area for improvement at a time. Encourage yourself in your marriage, and encourage others to improve their performance step by step rather than trying to tackle too much at once. Give yourself and your spouse room for feedback, both positive and negative, in any area you are working on. Let there be constant progress in your marriage. Never be satisfied that you are there already.

People need to know that you are doing well by your showing the example of your marriage. From time to time, share your testimonies of areas you have improved. Show you're serious about improvement. Constantly evaluate your marriage performance and involve yourself in growth. Encourage your wife to observe and evaluate your performance. Once everyone sees that excellence is everyone's concern, you're on the road to success. Participate in marriage seminars or programs as a form of evaluating your marriage, sharing experiences with others, especially those who have been longer married than you. I have the example of my senior pastor and others in the church who have been married for over thirty years, I am just over halfway along in that journey, so I have much to learn from their experience. It is working well.

As we learn from Ephesians 4:11–13, to move towards the "fullness of Christ" is to succeed in the work of your marriage and also create a balance for your ministry. Success does not necessarily equal something large. The largest is not the best; the loudest is not the best; and the flashiest is not the best—but neither are they the worst. Success equals excellence, and the best is showing the excellence of God in all that we do, particularly concerning our marriage. As we are Christians, the first thing people look at is our marriage. Whoever we are, wherever we are, with whatever we have or do, people will judge our marital union and see if it meets all these standards.

We are what we repeatedly do. Excellence then is not an act but a habit. Remember, an excellent church produces excellent people. The same goes for marriage; an excellent marriage is as attributable to excellent people.

CHAPTER 21

Can Marriage Be Perfect?

Is it possible to have a "perfect marriage"? Some people believe so, and some argue that it is impossible to have a perfect marriage. Those who argue against the idea of perfection postulate the idea of sinlessness, which is something expected of the believer. Others hold to the possibility of perfection but remember human frailty. To them, forgiveness is a continual necessity as individuals grow in their capacity to love and respond to the Lord. All these arguments are true and correct. I want to simply put it out there that you can work towards being perfect in your marriage with the understanding that the One who established the institution is perfect.

God never creates what is not perfect. Even the creation of humankind was adjudged by God to be very good and perfect. Man was made complete, but we know the rest of the story: when man sinned, he became imperfect. If man would stay within the confines of marriage, yes, we could experience a perfect marriage here on earth and the ultimate marriage of the Lamb of God with his people as a promise of a new kingdom where there is no imperfection, a New Jerusalem and a new earth, and a street fitted with gold.

Marriage is actually a practical training ground where we learn to be perfect—learning to live together as one, correcting our mistakes, and forgiving one another in the process. Marriage is a school of love where there are constant acts of forgiveness and learning.

- "There is no fear in love. But perfect love drives out fear, because fear has to do with punishment. The one who fears is not made perfect in love" (1 John 4:18).
- "There is not a righteous man on earth who does what is right and never sins" (Ecclesiastes 7:20).

God is perfect. His way, unveiled in his Word, is perfect, and by arming the believer with strength, God completely equips him or her for a righteous walk. But human beings are "perfect" only in the sense that David and Job were. Each of these men loved God and responded to him as each knew him, yet each was flawed before God restored them to his glory.

- "He is the Rock, his works are perfect, and all his ways are just. A faithful God who does no wrong, upright and just is he" (Deuteronomy 32:4).
- "As for God, his way is perfect; the word of the Lord is flawless. He is a shield for all who take refuge in him" (Deuteronomy 32:4).

Jesus was made perfect: As for Jesus himself, he was made perfect in the sense of having been fully equipped for his saving ministry.

- "And, once made perfect, he became the source of eternal salvation for all who obey him" (Hebrews 5:9).
- "For the law made nothing perfect, and a better hope is introduced, by which we draw near to God" (Hebrews 7:19).
- "For the law appoints as high priests men who are weak; but the oath, which came after the law, appointed the Son, who has been made perfect forever" (Hebrews 7:28).
- "Because by one sacrifice he has made perfect forever those who are being made holy" (Hebrews 10:14).

Becoming Perfect

The perfect human being is not a sinless paragon. The New Testament makes it clear that "we all stumble in many ways" (James 3:2). We realize that saints remain sinners. John says bluntly, "If we claim to be without sin, we deceive ourselves and the truth is not in us" (1 John 1:8). God deals with our failures by extending forgiveness and cleansing as we come to him (1 John 1:9). So "perfection" is not sinlessness. Therefore, if we come into marriage with this understanding, what sin could be there in the marriage that we cannot forgive? No sin. And let us not be blind to the fact that God will give us the grace to endure and to love one another. So when there is sin, ask God to give you the heart to be open to forgiveness when the other asks for it. Don't you expect to be forgiven yourself when you ask for forgiveness? Therefore, be willing to give forgiveness to someone else when it is asked of you.

We also find out that God holds out an exciting prospect for us. We can be "perfect" in the biblical sense of achieving our potential as husband and wife. Matthew records Jesus's words to all those who yearn to experience God's kingdom. We are to love our enemies and pray for our persecutors, as God the Father sends rain and sunshine on both the evil and the good. "Be perfect," Jesus concluded, "as your heavenly Father is perfect" (Matthew 5:48). God fulfils his divine potential and the potential of his love in his treatment of the wicked. As his children now, we are to fulfil our potential as Christians by loving even our enemies. In a marriage, it is a union of two persons who profess love towards each other. Don't allow the love in you to turn to wickedness. I have read enough ugly stories of a husband and a wife killing each other over insincerity or cheating and unforgiveness.

James says the same thing in the scripture. The person who controls his tongue has reached maturity. He achieves his potential as a Christian, and so in that sense, he is a perfect person.

- "You must be blameless before the Lord your God" (Deuteronomy 18:13).
- "Be very strong; be careful to obey all that is written in the Book of the Law of Moses, without turning aside to the right or to the left" (Joshua 23:6).
- "But your hearts must be fully committed to the Lord our God, to live by his decrees and obey his commands, as at this time" (1 Kings 8:61).
- "And over all these virtues put on love, which binds them all together in perfect unity.
- I can candidly suggest that you start working towards perfection in your marriage knowing God is in the center of it" (Colossians 3:14).

Marriage is a school of love where there is the constant act of forgiveness.

CHAPTER 22

Communication in Marriage

Having gone through the wedding ceremony and settled down to married life, you need tips on some of the things that will help your marriage work well. According to a good premarriage counselling handbook I read, written by Alan and Donna Goerz, here is a description of marriage. "A marriage is like being given a large mansion with many rooms to be used and enjoyed." But in many marriages you find the couple living in only a few rooms that can be opened easily. The rest of the house is full of locked doors. There is, however, a master key that will open every door and let the rooms be used and enjoyed. That key is good communication. I know so far you have been communicating, or else you would not be married, but there is a new form of communication that needs to be developed now.

The first danger we need to prevent against is that of following a family pattern in communication. We tend to communicate like our parents did. I provide some illustrations here on how our parents used to communicate. Let us be honest with our answers as a test to prepare for our effective communication skills with one another.

1. How did your father let your mother know that he was not pleased about something she had done or something she had not done well?

a. Shouted at her
b. Threatened her
c. Beat her
d. Refused to eat what she cooked
e. Gave her the silent treatment or left the house
f. Explained/discussed with her what he did not like
g. Complained to someone else (a family member, a neighbour, a friend)
h. I never saw my father displeased with my mom

2. How did your mother let your father know that she was not pleased about something he had done or said?

a. Gave him the silent treatment
b. Complained to someone else (a family member, a neighbour, a friend)
c. Refused to cook what he liked or when he wanted to eat
d. Shouted at him
e. Threatened him
f. Explained/discussed with him what she did not like
g. I never saw my mother displeased with my dad

3. How did your father communicate with you when you were a teenager in his home?

a. He gave orders and expected prompt obedience.
b. He discussed matters with me.
c. He asked after my opinion.
d. He seldom communicated with me.
e. He communicated in other ways.

4. How did your parents let you know they were not happy with your behaviour as a teenager?

a. By shouting and threatening
b. By beating me
c. By taking away my privileges
d. By giving me extra work to do
e. By talking the matter through with me
f. By ignoring me
g. By other means

These are all forms of communication with consequences.

I am sure that your answers will surprise you. My personal experience at home was that my parents communicated less; it was more that my dad gave orders to my stepmums. It didn't go down well many times; there were conflicts just because of the lack of effective communication. This comment is not judgemental but factual.

There are a few more questions on my list for you to answer:

5. How did your parents let you know they were pleased with your behaviour or achievements as a teenager?

a. By words of praise or appreciation
b. By gifts
c. By touch (a hug, an arm around the shoulder, a handshake)
d. By saying, "Why don't you do that well all the time?"

| e. They never seemed to notice |
| f. In other ways |

Having made these observations in communication, you should talk with each other about the similarities and differences in your families' ways of communicating. This is your first step towards understanding how best you should communicate with each other in the marriage.

Share with each other how each of these ways of communicating made you feel (e.g. secure, happy, loved, understood, valued, angry, afraid, rejected, disappointed).

Discuss how you would like to communicate with each other, even when you start having children. You must agree on which form of communication is best suited for your marriage.

Some tips on communication:

Listen

In a marriage, it is easy to determine how often the partners talk, but it is difficult to determine who is listening. You have been talking together about many things so far, but how would you rank your listening capability?

- Are you a good listener?
- Are you an excellent listener?
- Are you a fairly good listener?
- Are you not very good at listening?
- Are you a poor listener?

Listening is something that occurs between both of you. There is no shame if you have to improve your listening ability, but you should be honest about it with your spouse. Ask your partner, "How can I become a better listener?" Talk less; it is not a talking competition in your marriage. What does the Bible say about listening? Together with your wife or husband, read the scriptures in Proverbs 18:3, 17; 21:11, 23; and 29:20; and James 1:19.

When we are truly listening, we are not thinking about what we are going to say next. Nor are we thinking about something else, or continuing to read the newspaper, or watching television. We are simply listening to the other person.

What is actually happening is one of the following:

- We are concentrating on the other person with the intention to hear what he or she is saying.
- We are concentrating on the other person with the intention to know how he or she is feeling.
- We are concentrating on the other person to know his or her thoughts.
- We are concentrating on the other person to know what is beneath the words, in his or her heart.
- And lastly we are concentrating to know what the Holy Spirit is saying to us.

127

Listening requires concentration to hear, understand, and comprehend what your spouse is saying.

In the early stages of your marriage, it may be tough to listen. It takes a lot of practice to learn how to listen well. When someone talks to you, practise listening and talking less. And listen well.

Talk

There are several levels of communication, as I mentioned earlier, and one of them is talking. I will examine four levels of talking as a guide for your marriage:

Level 1—Talking very little. Body language is preferred over words to communicate. Body language sends a message. For a happily married couple, this can represent perfect confirmation in each other's presence. However, this kind of communication, if used for extended periods, will cause the breakdown of the relationship.

Level 2—Talking about facts, figures, and other such things. We share information and facts about the day or about other people, but we need to be careful how we bring those talks into our marriages. Try to leave office matters at the office, and if it is not of interest to your spouse, don't push it down his or her throat. Sometimes this falls into the category of the sin of gossip or slander of another person. Normally we don't talk about how we feel about the information; rather, we talk about the persons involved. The information may be useful. If so, take it to heart, and leave out the rest.

Level 3—Talking about your ideas and judgements/decisions. This is the first step in real communication because here you have to make decisions, come up with ideas, and make judgements about certain matters. There is no hiding from this level, but many people prefer to revert to level 1 or level 2 because it seems safe there. If what I say is made of fun, or if I don't feel accepted, many times I want to retreat, but really I should talk about it or communicate with my spouse instead of resorting to permanent silence. I advise the same for you.

Level 4—Sharing feelings and emotions. This form of talking is better as it brings out your thoughts. It is the step of sharing who you really are with your spouse. This is a form of complete mental, emotional, and personal communication. All deep relationships are based on absolute openness and honesty. It is the "naked and unashamed" relationship Genesis 2:25 talks about. Such communication is a precious treasure to have, and it must be handled with care in the marriage.

Note that we often tend towards either intellectual-based communication or towards emotional-based communication. Which do you prefer? Your acting like a friend and growing in oneness means you value your spouse's perspectives and feelings no matter what is written in the communication books. Are you willing to share both your thoughts and feelings with the other person unconditionally? Again, communication has nothing to do with your level of education. One spouse may be a PhD holder and the other a college dropout. If you are married, you need to find common ground for communication and make it effective too.

Another form of communication you need to consider in the marriage relates to time management: Of course it was easy when you were alone to plan and manage your time, but how best do you manage time now? In my marriage, management of time is often our most challenging issue. I need to prepare my wife one or two hours in advance if we have to go out together. She needs more time, I guess like many women, to prepare herself. In the early years of our marriage, I would get upset while waiting for her, but I have come to get used to it. I've learnt a better way of hurrying her along by making sure she starts by taking a shower and getting dressed first. Then I don't need to wait too long.

A marriage is like being given a large mansion with many rooms to be used and enjoyed.

Our time together needs to be planned with the children and other engagements in mind.

Trust is a very vital organ in communication, and it affects many things in the marriage, Trust is built on your commitment to these things, such as listening from your heart, loving your spouse just the way he or she is, putting his or her needs before your own, working on forgiveness, and not dwelling on past mistakes, realizing that divorce is not an option. Always be determined to find a solution. Where you cannot find a solution yourselves, seek help outside of the marriage.

Lack of truth is also a vital tool in quickly destroying a marriage or any form of relationship. Where there is no truth, there is the opposite: a lie. Nothing destroys a relationship faster than a lie. What does the Bible say about lies? Read Proverbs 6:16–19; John 8:44; Colossians 3:9–10; and Revelation 21:8.

On the other hand, being truthful is rewarding as the scripture says in John 14:6; Ephesians 4:15; 2 John 1, 3; and 3 John 3–4.

You have to be determined from the very beginning, before God and humankind, that you will not lie to your spouse ever—and if it does happen, you must come clean with it. If you have lied to your friend about something, confess it to him or her. You may think your spouse will never find out, but his or her spirit already knows, and he or she will be cautious about trusting you again in the future.

Confession will cause the bridge of trust to be rebuilt and fellowship to be restored. Many marriages are damaged beyond repair because of lies. An added advantage is found in James 4:6–10: confession lets us humble ourselves, then God starts to release amazing grace into our lives and our situations. Then our marriage will begin to enjoy a new lease of life.

CHAPTER 23

Conflict Management in Marriage

What are the reasons conflict may arise in your marriage? This is a good question. A simple answer I will give you for now is that you need conflict in your marriage if it is to work well. Conflict is a form of test of your resolution to either make your marriage work or else break it apart. Because of the differences between the two of you, there will be conflicts. If you were both the same, you wouldn't need each other in the first place. I imagine there are some conflicts arising from your respective family backgrounds, your values, your desires, your perspectives, your needs, your demands, and your wants—and many more factors to be discovered in the marriage.

Another thing that can bring conflict is sin, for instances unfaithfulness, pride, selfishness, anger, fear, frustration, hurt, insecurity, a need for control, arrogance, hypocrisy, and self-centeredness. None of these are virtues, but if one of them does show up in marriage and brings conflict, you have to learn how to deal with this monster.

Conflict is not a bad thing. What is bad is the way we go about dealing with our differences of opinion, our differing perspectives, and our different needs. Conflict can lead to greater understanding, better communication, growth, and change in our lives. It can also result in misunderstanding, anger, silence, distance, and a refusal to let God bring the right change to our lives.

What we need to deal with is how we handle conflicts. I will suggest a few points; you may discover more in your marriage. Take note of them, and begin to work on them immediately. The following are natural ways of handling conflict, but they all amount to a wrong approach:

The "I Must Win" Posture

I am in the right. I must be in charge. I must have the last word. This approach will kill communication and eventually the relationship. The marriage is under threat of collapse if the couple do not seek help very soon. You may win and protect your pride by adopting this attitude, but you damage the pride of your spouse and you lose the closeness and respect of your wife or husband. The "I" or "me" factor needs to be dealt with, or it will bring conflict in your marriage.

The "I Withdraw" Posture

I back off or out when a disagreement begins. You have kept the peace, but you have buried your own needs and have deprived your partner of your perspective, ideas, and opinions, which God may have given to you. The distance between you will increase. You are also teaching your partner that your ideas and needs are more important and that he or she can just have whatever you give instead of your seeking his or her opinion too.

The "I'll Negotiate" Posture

I give up something to gain something. This may not build oneness and openness in your marriage. You remain on opposite sides of the fence and are driving in different directions instead of coming into agreement and oneness.

The "I'll Manipulate or Use Blackmail" Posture

I will get what I want by making threats; bringing up past mistakes or issues; becoming angry or emotional over every little thing in the marriage; or withholding from my partner (e.g. money, sex, food, closeness, or talk) in order to make my point known or get it across to my partner.

In your own discussions, you may discover other areas of conflict I have not mentioned in *Getting to Know You.* I can assure you that now that you live together, you have the ability identify these areas of conflict even better. There are godly ways of handling conflict. For every problem, there is a solution—and we can find it in the Word of God.

1. There are times when you must yield. Just for peace to reign, you make some issues not as important as the other person makes them out to be. "It is not so important to me, but it is important for you, so let us reason together on it." Simply put, this is known as finding common ground.
2. When the other person does not see the value in what you are saying, the problem is probably your manner of presentation. Or perhaps the other person has not considered it the way you have presented it. Because of the points, the other person ultimately comes to agree with you. We can see the example of this in Acts 11.
3. When a husband has carefully listened to his wife, when he has prayed with sincerity and openness to hear from God and he still believes they should go with his decision, then I encourage the other partner to go along with the decision because it is in the best interests of the marriage. Many times my wife has trusted my decision as her husband and has accepted my opinion. Again, it does not make her a loser or weaker in the decision-making.

4. Most wives, if these conditions are met, will be able to yield to their husbands' authority and trust God for the outcome (1 Corinthians 11:3; 1 Peter 3:5). The couple needs to see their perspective as planting the seeds of thought and giving God time to grow those seeds.

Conflict is a form of testing your resolution to make your marriage work or else break it.

Agreement

Marriage is between two persons, meaning that they constantly have to reach agreement in all that they do together. Never intend or plan to make a decision for the other person without his or her knowledge. If you do this, you are inviting trouble into your marriage. If you are not sure what the person likes or wants, simply ask to avoid making a wrong choice. A man once told me he had tried to buy underwear for his wife as a surprise gift, but unfortunately they did not fit. Rather than the wife appreciating the gesture, she asked him, "Is this the size of your ex-lover?" Although she said it in a joking manner, her reply offended him. Ask her for size if you do not know it. Otherwise, your wife won't appreciate such a surprise.

Sometimes we think agreement means that one wins and the other loses. This is not the case. Genesis 1:21 shows us that it is usually not either or both. Oneness isn't the same as sameness. It is bringing two different people together to form a whole. This is very important to remember in times of conflict, for example child-rearing. Make time to read the following scriptures: John 17:21 and 17:23; and Matthew 18:19.

Rules

There are standard rules guiding marriage. I have read of the stupid behaviour and action of wife-beating as a husband's form of showing love to his spouse. That act is barbaric and stupid. There is no place in the Word of God where it is prescribed to beat your wife. Wife-beating is not a form of showing love to your spouse; rather, it is a form of abuse that should be condemned and punishable under the law.

I will give you some tips that will help you in your marriage as you seek to keep it holy and pure. These are simple principles that you do not need to go to school to learn. There are things you must never do in your marriage; this is for the husband as well as for the wife:

1. Never hit your spouse or throw a punch at your spouse (hands are to be used to love, caress, protect, and reassure).
2. Never call yourself names ("foolish", "worthless", "lazy", "idiot", etc.). The person you are calling those names is yourself. You married the person and have become one, so indirectly you are calling yourself an idiot for marrying him or her.
3. Never use words like *never* or *always*. Those words aren't true. If your spouse says that he or she cannot stop engaging in this bad habit of yours, know that he or she can if only you will help him or her and provide support in the recovery effort.

133

4. Never say "You are just like your mother [or father]" in a derogatory way. This is dishonouring the parents and implying the other person cannot change or is not properly trained. That may not be the case. But if it is the case, the person is now your spouse, so you must find ways to solve the problems rather than playing the blame game, which does not help your marriage.

5. Never say "It's your entire fault," because it rarely is! It takes two to tango. If there is a problem, something created or started it. Something fuelled it. You have to agree to work together to solve the problem. I have heard some women say, "My husband does not love me anymore," meaning that the husband once loved his wife. What happened that caused your husband to stop loving you? If you can identify the problem, it is not too difficult to find a solution. First always look to yourself before pointing your finger at your spouse.

6. Never refuse to talk about it. Probably this is the worst situation you can find yourself in, in your marriage, when the other person does not want to talk about something. No matter what it is, talk about it before you take stupid action or make a stupid decision. To keep the peace, you may say, "I am not ready to talk about it yet or right now. Can we talk later?" (You may agree to talk later that night after dinner, or some other agreed-upon time, but ensure it is no longer than twenty-four hours, i.e. within a day). Don't use this as an excuse not to talk about the issue or as an escape which lets you keep avoiding the other person so that he or she hopefully stops bothering you about the subject. Talk about it, please.

   Another idea for postponement is to wait until you aren't so angry anymore and God has given you perspective. It is important not to use silence as a weapon of defence or revenge instead of talking to your spouse.

7. Never bring up the past. The matter was resolved and forgiven and in the past. I hear people say, "Yes, I have forgiven, but I cannot forget the past." Well, whatever the view you take, the past many times comes back to hurt you, never to heal the wound, so I still suggest that you leave the past to the past. Micah 7:19 says that God casts all our sins into the depths of the sea. I don't know how many of us can swim deep into the sea to search for whatever has been thrown there or lost during a sailing adventure. It is practically impossible. Someone added to the scripture, "And he posts a No Fishing sign."

8. Never say "I am leaving." Even if you don't mean it, you have communicated clearly that you are willing to break your covenant, and this gives a wrong signal to your partner. If such a word comes out of your mouth, you give your partner room to conjure up ideas or even make conclusions. It destroys trust and will make reconciliation very difficult, which puts the marriage in danger.

The following things are my suggestions. They're some of the things you can do. I use this acronym: DADDD.

1. Determine

The couple must be determined. Probably a better word is *committed*. The couple must realize that they are each a side of the same coin. There is no difference between the two, knowing that God's perspective is the one that matters in the marriage. The two must be committed to listening to each other's words, feelings, and most importantly hearts; they should share their hearts' intent sincerely and openly.

2. Agree

Again, the two cannot differ too much in many things in their marriage if they want to keep their marriage. As Proverbs 15:23 suggests, they must agree on how to deal with their problems and find solutions together. Can the two work together without coming into agreement? Agree, agree, and agree all the time.

3. Define

Open discussion, open agreement, and sincere openness to the areas of agreement. Use the same yardstick for areas of disagreement.

4. Discuss

It would be perfect if both of you were talking and discussing each matter affecting your family. Each of you should make open suggestions and be given equal opportunity to respond. Any biblical principle that is very clearly applied to the marriage should be accepted and applied. In your discussion, always see possible solutions. Make brainstorming decisions, which means you look at all aspects of each possibility—the good, the bad, the weird, and the wonderful—and that you keep coming up with ideas until you find the one that is *right*.

5. Decide

Together, implement your decision. If you cannot come to agreement, or if one partner starts using foul words or being violent, get help, please. Never stay in an abusive marriage. It could hurt you. And the longer it continues, the worse it becomes. Do not go to a family member (they will be offended at your spouse long after you have worked things out and have forgotten about the fight!). Don't go to a friend (for similar reasons; besides, he or she may tell another friend, who will tell someone else, and so on).

Do go to a man or woman of God, for example your pastor or a godly counsellor, who has knowledge of God's Word and who knows of ways to help you.

Decision-making is very important in your marriage. Many times you cannot make the correct decision alone; you need your spouse's input to make the right decision. "What type of car will be good for the family now that we are expecting our first child?" Your partner will suggest a spacious car to carry the baby wagon and allow room for a helper, and not a two-door car for the two of you. Simple things like this need to be decided together. A couple one time called me because they had had a dispute. What was the problem? The wife, trying to help improve the family's chance of getting a good mortgage to buy a house, decided to change her job but without telling her husband. She went for the job interview and secured the job. Upon reaching home, she broke the good news to her husband, but he was not excited. Rather he was angry. "When did all of this happen without my knowledge?"

Even though the intention was good, the manner in which it was done was not pleasant in terms of the marriage. That night the husband refused to eat her meal out of anger. The next morning, I spoke to both of them and helped to iron out the differences. I made both of them realize that they have to decide everything together in the marriage because they are one.

Decision-making is very important in your marriage. Many times you cannot make the correct decision alone. You need your spouse's input to make the right decision.

CHAPTER 24

A Radiant Wife

A wife is a fragrance. She needs to show love, happiness, and inner beauty. These qualities are guaranteed to attract her to her husband. I want you men to carefully read this, as it will help you to create the wife of your dreams. I am sure that you, like every man, have a perfect picture or image of the wife of your dreams, but many times you never find that wife—because she does not exist. You have to make her or create her. I am going to give you some tips and information to help you discover that radiant wife:

1. Allow God to cleanse your wife by his Word. It is the responsibility of the man to bring his wife into the presence of God. Maybe this will help you begin to understand why God gave the task of being the head (leader) to the man and not the woman. It is the man's task to help his wife find time with God, even if it means taking charge of the children or helping out at home with domestic activities so she can have time to be in the presence of God. Complement her by studying, reading, and praying together from the Word of God. In fact, the ideal situation is when the husband reads the Bible to his wife as a love-sharing activity within the family, long before the children arrive. And when you do have children, you continue in similar manner. This is according to Ephesians 5:25. The husband should make sure that he works with his wife to adjust to the needs of the children and the time factor in raising them.

2. Consistently praise your wife for any godly characteristics you see in her. This is an expression of the fruits of the Spirit spoken about in Proverbs 31:30. Praise her. This calls attention to certain qualities of her character. For instance, tell her, "You showed such a great patience when …" In this regard, you have to differentiate between praise and flattery. Praise has to do with factual and truthful information, whereas flattery involves lies and untruthfulness; you don't mean what you say. Flattery will not motivate your wife; rather, it will discourage her. Therefore, concentrate on her inner qualities that bring lasting beauty. For instance, motivate her to have pride in her physical features, which

will change with age and bring insecurity as she compares herself to other women. My wife is over fifty-five years of age and has some grey hairs beginning to appear, but I keep assuring her that she remains my ever-beautiful wife with grey hair. With me, she does not need to colour her hair. I just love her the way she is. Her beauty is within.

3. Help your wife abolish her secret fears. God warns us over and over in the Bible not to fear. When we entertain fears and worries, we give Satan the opportunity to ask God for permission to carry them out. Read Job 3:25. Fear is not of God. "God has not given us a spirit of fear, but of power, love and of a sound mind" (2 Timothy 1:7). Your love towards your wife will help her cast out her fears (2 John 4:18). Let your words not be self-serving or accompanied with wrong motives. Therefore you need to share your fears with her too, letting her encourage you with the Word of God. That will give her the courage to share her fears with you in the same manner.

4. Build trust by being a one-woman man. If a wife fears her husband will take another woman, then her fears may cause her to take action which will damage the spirit of the marriage. If she sees or senses that her husband is delighting in the friendship or company of other women, she will experience feelings of jealousy, envy, insecurity, resentment, and rejection unless she is carried along to allay all fears or suspicions.

5. Treat your wife as special, and she will feel and act special. I have heard men complain of their wives, saying they are no longer beautiful or that they no longer dress nicely. Take your wife to a nice fashion house and let them do a makeover of her wardrobe at your expense; you will get your wife back. Learn good manners, put your wife first before the children, and be proud of her both in private and in public. Do not let your family members or friends meet the needs of your wife. No matter how well my family members cook, I eat the meals my wife provides me, and she knows I love to eat at home.

I sometimes get our children jealous by the way I treat their mom. They tell me we are behaving like two little kids in love. That is a great compliment after twenty years together.

6. Encourage your wife to seek fulfilment through her God-given responsibilities. Bearing children, is the first command of God in Genesis 1:28. See also 1 Timothy 5:14. I met a woman in my early years in Europe who was dating a black man, and she told me that she did not want to have children. I asked her what the response of the black guy was, and she said that he walked out on her, unable to understand why a woman would not want to bear children. I told her I shared the same view, as it is God's command. If for no other reason than it is beyond our human understanding, husband and wife should be fruitful by bearing children. A wife and mother enjoys teaching her children. As we learn from Deuteronomy 4:9, 6:7, if you as the father delegate to others the teaching of your children, you must retain the overall responsibility. Galatians 4:1–2 tells us that if God does not give you natural children after you have made all humanly possible efforts, consider the possibility that God has children for you to adopt and raise up for his honour and glory. See Exodus 2:10; Esther 2:7; Romans 8:15–16; Galatians 4:5–7; and Ephesians 1:3–6. These children are going to become your spiritual children as you invest in them

and teach them, train them, and encourage them in God's ways (2 Timothy 1:2). (To learn about Timothy's real parents, you can read Acts 16:1–2.) All of this information on children is for the woman to realize that she is to keep the home front (1 Timothy 1:2) and advance the goals of the home (Proverbs 31). It is a huge task God has given the wife in the home. If the wife is able to effectively carry out these tasks, then she can serve the purpose of God in the community/church under the leadership and direction of her husband (Galatians 3:28).

7. Refuse to damage the spirit of your marriage through these destructive deeds:
    a. Failing to love your wife.
        This is probably your greatest sin. Why did you marry her if you don't love her? Don't fail to honour, respect, and cherish your wife more than every other woman, and more than any job, hobby, or family member, in your life (Genesis 2:23–24; 1 Corinthians 7:32–33; Ephesians 5:25).
    b. Neglect to provide your wife spiritual leadership (2 Chronicles 26:5).
    c. Short-changing her in moves within the family without adequate time to mentally prepare herself and think through all the details of that change.
        Take for instance moving to another location or city. You may like the idea, but does your wife share the same view? The transition may bring unnecessary stress upon your marriage, and you don't want that, so talk about it before acting.

8. Do not make comparisons with other women. Wives are extremely alert and sensitive to what their husbands look at, and when a woman notices her husband looking admiringly or lustfully at another woman (including in pictures, in movies, in magazines, or on the Internet), she feels deep pain and rejection (Proverbs 4:23–25). Therefore, never compare her with other women such as your mother or sister; if you do, you convey a message of failure to her, causing her guilt and frustration. You don't want that in your marriage.

9. Be self-disciplined. *Discipline* is a word that often we do not talk about in marriage as we expect it to automatically happen, but discipline is an action word. We have to do it. For instance, anger damages marriage and relationships with children, and it is an act arising from a lack of discipline (Proverbs 25:28). Often, anger is a result of frustration arising from lack of communication or from assuming that communication was clear when it really wasn't. Anger is a result of moral impurity; therefore, self-discipline is also required during times when sexual intimacy is inappropriate or medically unwise. You must not rape your wife, or any other woman for that matter, no matter the circumstances. Also, show discipline with regard to the use of family money. It is important that you manage the family finances properly as your financial health affects the health of your marriage.

10. Recognize your wife's little efforts to please you, and praise her for them. What annoys a wife and puts her off is when she feels unappreciated in a marriage, particularly if it is her husband who is failing to show his appreciation. Wives are very detailed. They will put special time, thought, and effort into some "little" things, preparing to surprise the family. If the husband does not notice and appreciate such an effort, the wife is disappointed; and when a husband is insensitive to the special things his wife does, he causes her to

become susceptible to admiration and praise from others, for example from other men or through being employed outside the family. No husband likes these consequences, so don't create them for yourself. Your wife may also lose her creativity and start showing signs of depression if you fail to acknowledge her efforts.

A wife is a fragrance.

11. Avoid correcting your wife in public. (Wives, this goes for you too.) Talk over your issues in private no matter what the problem or matter is, not even in front of the children or other members of the family at home. This includes talking about your problems with parents, who can easily take up an offence which they will carry long after the two of you have settled the issue and forgotten about it.

12. Take your wife's suggestions and opinions as very important. Wives are more sensitive on issues; therefore, give your wife a listening ear and an understanding mind. Even if your wife doesn't understand all the details, such as those of a business decision, she will be sensitive in her spirit to the people involved, the ways of God, or the timing of the decision. It is not wise to move ahead until there is oneness of spirit (Philippians 2:2–1; Corinthians 1:10). And if you don't carefully listen to your wife, she will be reluctant to share her insights and feelings with you in the future. God will often give a wife special insight. Seek God together until you can reach a decision which both have peace about in your spirits (Philippians 4:7). Many men have made disastrous decisions because they failed to listen to the warnings of their wives (Matthew 27:19).

13. Learn godly ways of training and disciplining the children. A child with motherly training is best-behaved, researchers have admitted. I beg to agree with this assertion. Fathers are to give training and discipline to the children. The wife is to execute the discipline by making sure the homework is done, that beds are tidy, that clothes are washed, and that domestic tasks are carried out. Mothers translate the commands into action steps (Proverbs 6:20–23). For example, a father will say, "I want you to keep your room clean." The mother will give directions on how to do it: "Let's put a box here to keep your toys in" or "Let's remove all these because Daddy will not like to see them sitting there." When a father gives a command and it is not done the way he wants it, many times it is the mother who takes the blame, so she wants to be on top of it. Taking a class in parenting or reading books on this subject will enable you to raise your children in godly ways.

14. Acknowledge when you fail or do wrong, and ask for forgiveness from your wife. There is nothing macho or manly about being wrong or failing in your task as a husband. I have been told that a father does not admit failure in the presence of his wife or children. Total rubbish. If you fail in your responsibility as a husband, be bold enough to admit your mistake, fault, or sin and to ask for forgiveness. Your wife and children will react to anything you do out of pride in a manner you will not appreciate or like; therefore, overcome the fear that you will lose respect or lose face with your wife or children. If you don't do the right thing, your wife and children will react to your pridefulness, and then you'll lose respect from them anyhow (James 4:6–10; 1 Peter 5:5–6). When a father reacts

in anger and does not apologize, the children will also develop anger and bitterness in their hearts (Ephesians 6:4). And again, when a father covers his sin, he brings unnecessary hardship on his family (Proverbs 28:13). Finally, when a husband continues to fail in his responsibilities, his prayers will not be answered (1 Peter 3:7). Therefore, forgive. It will bring oneness of spirit and agreement in prayer again, and the marriage will thus be able to endure to the end.

I am sure every man has a perfect picture or image of the woman of his dreams. But many times he never finds that woman because she does not exist. He has to make her or create her.

CHAPTER 25

Practical Marital Experiences

Story of Godfrey and Loretta

Godfrey Joseph Titi, a young man who joined our church alongside his elder brother, Pastor Kevin Omondi, was a man who loved the Lord. Neither Godfrey nor Loretta was married when they joined us. Godfrey was a quiet guy who did not talk much. One afternoon I received a phone call from a fellow pastor in Kisumu, Pastor Eric. After an exchange of pleasantries, he asked me if I knew a brother called Godfrey Titi. "Yes" was my response. I'd known Godfrey as a dear brother in the Lord who attended services faithfully, and he was a tither in the church, so his name was familiar to me. The pastor told me that he would like to set up a meeting with me because this young man was interested in a daughter of his at his church. Her name was Loretta Achieng. I agreed to meet with the pastor. The next step was to talk to Godfrey myself.

The meeting with Pastor Eric set in motion *Getting to Know You*. He had the idea that we as a church were not doing enough to help young people in their walk towards marriage. There were too many teenage pregnancies in the churches. When the young women were asked to name the men who were responsible for their pregnancies, they just laughed without saying a word. Many of them did not know who was responsible because they kept multiple guys. I was delighted to see a pastor making such an effort to contact me to find out about a brother in my church who was interested in a woman in his church. It was not a common move.

So I took Godfrey aside to ask him what was happening and if indeed he did know a woman called Loretta. He admitted to knowing her and said that he was interested in her. I asked him if he had met her pastor. He said he had, and that the pastor actually requested for my telephone number from him, which he gladly gave to him. I told Godfrey I was going to have a talk with the pastor in case Godfrey had to prepare me for anything I needed to know. Godfrey said nothing, just repeating that he was interested in a sister in the other church. He told me he liked her and the relationship was just a friendship for now, but he asked me to pray along with him for God's revelation.

I found this approach very interesting. I hope pastors reading *Getting to Know You* will learn a lesson from this development. There is nothing wrong if someone from another church is interested in any member of your church. Your responsibility is to guide them on the right path to go but not to stop them or say why you are looking into another church; you must only find someone from within your church. I have a spiritual son who found love in another church headed by another pastor who was willing to give a daughter to us in marriage; it was the first time I had experienced this type of union with two churches agreeing to work together to see our son and daughter happily married thereafter. Amazingly it worked.

Once I became convinced through the Holy Spirit that Godfrey and Loretta were making the right decision, they had my blessing, and we gave them all the support to make the wedding a success. I met Pastor Eric at his church office, along with one of his staff, and we discussed these two young people who professed to love each other. I discovered in the course of the discussion that Loretta was a committed and devoted Christian in her church. She was a Sunday school teacher and an intercessor in the church. Once she had informed her pastor of a man making advances towards her; the pastor asked her about the man and the church he attended. I also gave a report of praise on Brother Godfrey. I promised the pastor to work closely with him on this subject and to give him a feedback. For close to three months, Pastor Eric and I worked together helping these two young people in making the right decision on their future together.

Both of them knew that their pastors where aware of their relationship. From that moment, we started praying together. Then counselling began for both of them, one session with me and another session with Pastor Eric. We compared notes. It is because of that experience I thought of writing *Getting to Know You*, which is now a reality.

One thing that I loved about Godfrey and Loretta was that they feared God and they were willing to go God's way. Many times I saw them together in church in their spare time, coming together and praying together for their relationship.

They informed us of all their plans. I continue to hold discussions with Loretta's pastor about her and Godfrey's relationship. It was not a problem to decide that the wedding would take place at Loretta's church and that both Pastor and I would officiate the wedding. It is so beautiful when we agree to work together for the common good of our church members, being that our churches are about our people. I led the groom and his family to the in-laws to request Loretta's hand in marriage and have the dowry paid in the traditional way. Subsequently there was nothing in the way to stop the couple from getting married. They tied the knot in 2011, and they are happily married now, blessed with children.

Pastor Kevin Omondi Weds Elizabeth

One of my sons, Pastor Kevin Omondi Owino, the senior brother of Godfrey, also went after a sister from another church, Dominion Chapel Church, Kisumu. Our churches were really fertile grounds; it was a show of the bond between our two churches. We had church activities together; we prayed together, worked together, and played together. Therefore, the people of each church were exposed to each other in a positive way.

Pastor Kevin used to attend the lunch hour services at Dominion Chapel Church because he was working in the city centre. It was closer, so it was better for him to attend the afternoon service there instead of travelling far to attend our services. I approved of his attending the lunch hour services at Dominion Chapel Church. Of course he soon found more than the Word of God interesting at the church. During his worship there, while doing some errands for the pastor, he met this sister who was working for the pastor at the church office. According to Pastor Kevin, on a few occasions, he helped her out, running some church errands in the city. Something developed, and before you knew it, there was love in the air. Pastor Kevin discovered a good rose in that church.

Once he informed me of his interest in the woman, I asked him to contact her pastor and let him know of the development and to seek the pastor's approval of Kevin's request to speak with her. Kevin came to inform me that he had done it. I in turn asked about the beautiful rose he had found in that church through the pastor who happened to be my neighbour and good friend (he is married to a Nigerian pastor sister as well). I wanted to know first-hand if the woman he was interested in was available for him to have. I asked him to invite her to come over and visit our church. She came a couple of times to join us after service or for our evening services. My wife and I had fellowship with her. We talked about their lives, and we discovered that both of them were already parents. They had children from previous relationships, but they were not married. This type of information is important to have as it helps during the counselling session. The partners in such a circumstance have to think it through if they intend to become one family. They would need to accommodate their children in the marriage if they were to become husband and wife. They went through pastoral counselling under the supervision of Dr George; his wife, Elizabeth Kennedy; and me.

It was a singing-couple-to-be. Elizabeth was a Praise and Worship member in her church, and my son Kevin used to lead the praise and worship in our church before I gave him another assignment in the church. After a year of dating, a period of getting to know each other better, Kevin and Elizabeth provided me with another colourful wedding ceremony in our church. Both Dr George Kennedy and I officiated the wedding. Elizabeth Achieng Odero and Kevin Omondi Owino got married on 4 December 2010, and the marriage is blessed today with more children. In fact, both husband and wife are now pastors and are pioneering a work in the city of Kisumu, Kenya.

My First Wedding Experience: Cliffe and Terry

These two, Cliffe and Terry, kick-started a series of weddings in my six-year sojourn in Kisumu, Kenya. I am very proud of these two for being good examples. Their marriage has endured many storms and has become brighter for all to see in Kisumu, Kenya, where they run their family business together.

Cliffe was a member of a church in Tom Mboya Estate, one of the biggest Pentecostal churches in Kisumu. His younger brother, Geoffrey, started with me and was a very helpful and efficient hand.

Once in a while, Cliffe visited our church. And I had gone to their family home, where they lived together. He had a live-in girlfriend, Terry Abong'o, and together they already had a daughter. I spoke with him, and he was open. I encouraged him to solemnize his relationship. He later decided to join our church since he was not committed on the other side. He attended a few of our services, and after a while, having decided that he liked the sermons and probably my personality, he decided to stay. I welcomed him. In the course of my talks with him, he decided to talk about his relationship and probably getting married. He also had the desire to serve God and work for God's kingdom, so I told him that it was time for him to do the right thing by officially asking for Terry's hand in marriage. He wanted to do it, but he was experiencing the usual fears of how to go about the wedding plans and arrangements. I promised that the church would assist him in the planning and execution of the wedding in such a way that it would not be a burden on his and Terry's resources. Of course Terry's parents were not happy that Cliffe had knowledge of their daughter before they were married. Her parents were church leaders, so their daughter's act was seen as disgraceful. Once Cliffe and Terry had professed their love for each other, I didn't want them to continue to live in sin. I was expecting that the union would be blessed of God.

I asked Cliffe to discuss the matter with his partner and his parents as soon as possible, saying that we would put together a wedding plan for them. His parents agreed, and they were thankful that I had taken the initiative for them. The next subject was the cost of the wedding. Cliffe was dead scared that it would be too expensive for him to cover. I advised him to plan the wedding within his budget, saying that we would have a colourful wedding and support him as a church. I accompanied him to visit his parents to fix the date when we would visit his in-laws and officially request for the hand of their daughter in marriage. The father was very blessed to see a pastor taking this initiative and to see church members doing the right thing before other church members so the latter could follow suit.

The parents of Terry, of course, were very strict and demanded that things be properly done. Terry had to return to the home of her parents, where she properly asked to be married. I guaranteed the families that with my presence there and with my being Cliffe's pastor, the couple would follow the plan of separation to the letter. The parents gave their approval for the marriage arrangement to go ahead. On 12 December 2009, I held my first wedding at Victory Outreach Kenya, for Cliffe Ombogo Oduor and Terry Millicent Abong'o. They were my first married couple in the church, blessed through my hands. Today they are blessed with two daughters and a son, and they are happily married and doing well in the Lord.

Their example is worthy of mention because they were already living together. They could have said, "It's a marriage already," like many others living in denial. They accepted that it was not right for them to be cohabitating, and they were willing to correct it before God. Both of them served under my leadership in the church until 2011, when I had to return to the Netherlands. Cliffe and Terry are doing well in their present church, and their pastor is full of praises for both of them.

George and Hellen

Pastor George Ochieng served under me in Kisumu, Kenya, before the political electoral crisis in 2008, at which point he left and moved to another city, where he started a church of its own. While working on that, he came to inform me that he had found a woman he wanted to marry, and he wanted me to be their counselling pastor and also officiate the wedding in Eldoret. It was such an honour to be found worthy to be trusted to guide Pastor George and his bride through the process. I visited him in Eldoret, and we spoke several times via the telephone. Finally a date was set for the marriage. With my wife and children, I spent the weekend in Eldoret to bless their wedding and officiate. I blessed their union on 27 November 2010. Today, Pastor George and Hellen Ochieng are the pastors of Shiloh Worship Center, Eldoret, Kenya.

My Last Wedding in Kenya: Tony and Emma

This was special to me because these two people were very special and close to my family. I saw the start of this relationship, through to the final chapter of their getting married. I saw the relationship from day one. Miss Emma Magwaro is a pretty young woman I first met on one of my early visits to Kisumu, Kenya, in 2005. She was very shy and not very talkative, but she was a very smart girl with a talent for singing. She was an orphan who had been raised by her uncle alongside his children. Many times she wept on my shoulder, but I encouraged her to keep pushing for the best in God. I saw a lot of potential in her. When I finally resumed as pastor of the church in Kisumu, she headed the Praise and Worship team of the church despite her age. She was willing to learn and was always smiling. About a year into our ministry in Kisumu, a young man joined us as a keyboardist, Anthony, who was also very lovable. Emma and Anthony worked together in the Praise and Worship team to bring it to a higher level. But after a time, I started to notice that they were always the last two to leave the church premises. They spent a lot of time in the open field talking. I sometimes wondered what they were talking about.

On several occasions, I unintentionally ran into them while driving home because both of them lived on the same route to my house. I don't think they wanted me to see them, but many times I saw them together. I grew suspicious. One day I confronted Anthony to ask him what was going on between him and Emma. He told me, "Nothing serious. We are just friends, Pastor. If anything more develops, I promise that you will be the first to know about it." I think their dating period was the longest I'd witnessed in Kenya, probably four years, although they were young, which is why I kept a close watch on their relationship.

After a time, I asked Emma the same question about what was happening between her and Anthony. She said it was just friendship and nothing more to it. I warned her of all the dangers of an unholy friendship, saying that to engage in such would affect her spiritual life and growth. In the second place, she was working for the Lord in his vineyard.

In the second year of their relationship, after they had spoken to each other, Brother Anthony finally came to me to admit that he was interested in Emma. He told me that he thought he loved her, and was considering developing the relationship towards marriage. From that moment on, I held regular counselling meetings with them and explained to them all the dos and don'ts in such a relationship. I was, from that point on, involved in the relationship, all the way up to his proposal to her on his birthday; his introduction to her family; the payment of the bride price; and finally the wedding itself. I faced a challenge with this relationship because the uncles of Emma who were to give her away in marriage were mostly Seventh-Day Adventists, so they objected to any wedding plans on Saturday, which for them was their Sabbath day. The couple-to-be was worried that I would not agree to have the wedding on a Sunday. They could not speak it to me, but when it came to my attention, I assured them that there was no problem with having the wedding on a Sunday, or any other day, as long as they could get their guests to attend on such a day.

Once their families and friends agreed that they would attend the wedding whenever we set the date, it was no problem to set the wedding date for a Sunday. We had a normal Sunday morning church service, and after that we started the church wedding at around 2 p.m. Amazingly, it was well attended. And it was very colourful. I was happy to be able to bless this union because the next day, I flew out of Kenya, having completed my missionary work after nearly six years. My first major assignment was to organize a wedding, and my last assignment was to conduct a wedding ceremony for my very faithful son and daughter in the church. I could not ask for more from God. Of my spiritual children, Emma and Anthony were two of the most charming. I love Emma and Anthony Alaka, and I continue to stay in contact with them in their marriage. They are blessed with two daughters and are doing well in the Lord.

All of these marriages, I have a responsibility towards the couples to ensure that their marriages abide. It is the same for many of you who have participated in one wedding or the other; do you still stay in touch with the couple? You have to. That was a marriage God had made possible for you to be a part of, and it is a privilege to ensure that the marriage is well and good.

Remembering their anniversaries and sending them your best wishes will always cause a couple to remember their commitment and their vows to one another.

Churches have the responsibility to help their members through the wedding procedures. Too many couples are afraid that it is too tedious and demanding, so they prefer to live together and pretend they are married. Living together is not the same as being married.

Working with these various pastors and churches, for me, made organizing weddings into something very beautiful and unifying, which I think gladdened the heart of God. With the modest success I had with weddings in my church, I became the wedding pastor, getting invitations to come and officiate weddings in Nairobi and other places.

Weddings in Nairobi, Naivasha, Eldoret, and Kisumu

I participated in and officiated another five weddings during my stay in Kenya. I enjoyed seeing two people coming together and becoming one. I feel I owe all these people who allowed me into their lives and permitted me to share their stories. I pray always that their marriages may endure to the very end of life. I continue to be part of their lives as many of them send me praise reports even though I do not ask for them.

I look forward to reuniting with them. When I do see them again, I will present them with a copy of *Getting to Know You* in Kenya while saying, "Thank you for sharing your lives with my wife and me during those beautiful six years in Kenya."

CHAPTER 26

Basic Needs of Husband and Wife

A few years ago, I was invited to speak at a marriage seminar in The Hague in the Netherlands; the topic was "What a wife expects from a husband". All the speakers were men, and the majority of the audience were women. The women were excited to hear from men of God, eager to learn what they had to say on this subject. I expected to see more men interested in knowing what their wives expected from them. I guess the men did not turn out because they feared they would be blamed or have a finger pointed at them. One speaker after the next outlined what wives expected from their husbands, all of them sharing great ideas and good words, but when it came to my turn, I presented what the needs are for husband and wife. I will share some of these needs with you in *Getting to Know You*. I made the declaration that whatever a wife expects from the husband, the husband expects the same back—no more, no less. It is a union of give and take, and no one person can give it all. I started with what a husband needs from a wife. I've made it into an eight-point summary so you can read it here. I know there are more needs, but this will be a good representation.

1. A husband needs a wife who respects him as a man (Ephesians 6:33). A wife may destroy the man by overexpecting her husband to meet her physical, mental, social, emotional, and spiritual needs. Never forget that both the husband and the wife must trust God as their first source of everything. If you are a wife, I suggest that you join forces with your husband to seek God's divine help rather than expecting your husband to know what you need and provide all you need. There may come a time when he is not capable of doing that; do not allow it to affect your affection for him. This will crush your husband's spirit. At the same time, a wife's godliness is a powerful guard against her husband's abusing her (1 Peter 3:1). Wife, don't take matters into your own hands. You may avoid temporary consequences by doing so, but in the long run, it will ultimately cause destruction. I would suggest that a wife learn the power of prayer first, according to James 5:16. Don't become

your husband's conscience, but wisely appeal to his conscience like Esther and then give him room to make decisions.

2. A husband needs a wife who accepts him as a leader and believes in his God-given responsibilities. A husband needs the assurance that his authority comes from God, and such assurance is only possible when the husband has a wife standing next to him. You see it with successful men, who bring their wives along with them and proudly display them. Husbands are to govern their wives, and the wives are to submit to their husbands. In fact, a wife's submission to her husband qualifies her husband for a church leadership position, and his leadership is an illustration of Christ to the church. He knows how to display loyalty when he makes mistakes or pressure increases because of his supporting wife—and loyalty can only be demonstrated in adversity.

3. A husband loves an appreciative wife, appreciating him in all his ways. A husband should show honesty, exhibit sincerity, walk in righteousness, speak and keep the truth, refuse to gossip, do no evil, take no offence, honour godly people, keep his promises, listen to his conscience, and fear the Lord. First Timothy 3:2–8 shows some characteristics of a good husband; wives, if your man has these, please appreciate him. Those qualities include a clear conscience, generosity, patience, spiritual alertness, wisdom, modesty, and hospitableness. A good husband has only one wife, is a peacemaker, desires to teach, is not covetous, is a good manager of the family, is not a drinker, is a hard worker, is a person who grows the church, and is disciplined. Let your husband hear you praise him to others without boasting.

4. A husband needs a wife who encourages him. Encouragement comes in various shapes and sizes. You may note down the encouragement needed in these few areas:

   a. Encourage him not to give up on God-given goals. However, realize that birth, death, and the fulfilment of the vision are part of God's purpose for your lives together.

   b. Encourage him to verbalize his deepest wishes and hold those in confidence that he treasures most as precious. Give him suggestions on how to implement his dreams, visions, and goals. Be part of his story from struggle to success.

   c. Encourage him by your patience and understanding during difficult times, during times of pressure, or amid postponements. Learn to accept difficult situations as part of God's ways, and do not give up or give your husband deadlines. Let him do what he must do in God's perfect will for your family.

   d. Encourage him by your expressed words, your pride in him, and your appreciation for his accomplishments.

   e. Encourage him by reminding him of the benefits of his leadership as a husband and trusting him.

   f. Encourage him by your attentiveness when he is talking either to you or to others. You could add more areas where you can be of encouragement to him; your husband will greatly appreciate it.

5. A husband needs a wife who will keep developing her inward and outward beauty and who continues growing in these areas: femininity, contentment, neatness, submissiveness,

diligence, softness, acceptance, patience, organization, discipline, dressing and attractiveness, hairstyle, and ultimately trust in God. I wouldn't want to spend time breaking it down for you, but you wives understand what I am talking about here. Be modest in your choice of clothes, hairstyle, and accessories. Pay attention to your body that you don't draw the attention of other men to your body. Forget whatever any other person says to you. What matters most is what your husband says. My wife often asks me, "Do you like my dress?" Once I say yes, she is satisfied. The home is a symbol to the world of a husband's wisdom, provision, and protection. Through the wife, there is nothing lacking in the home. A quiet spirit is a conquering spirit over fear and worries. This is a quality that a woman should possess, allowing her to win the heart of the most difficult husband.

6. A husband needs a wife who can lovingly appeal to him when he is going beyond his limitations and who can wisely respond to those who question his ideas or motives. If your husband is a leader of people, either in business or ministry, then he needs a totally understanding wife who is in right standing with God.

Whatever a wife expects from the husband, the husband expects the same back, no more, no less.

She can use the right basis for appeal, his reputation, his goals, and his authority. When I was a pastor in Kenya, some people tried to seek my wife's sympathy in order to reach me. They asked her to influence some of my decisions, but she never did. She stood with me, knowing the decision was right, and she conveyed the right attitude so we were in right timing and accurate in our facts. Kindly apply these principles in appealing to your husband and to help others to understand your husband's perspective. Build appreciation for his motives even if his ideas turn out to be wrong. Learn from the examples in the Bible, such as Sarah's obedient spirit (1 Peter 3:1–7), Esther's wise appeals (Esther 5–9), and Ruth's loyal spirit (Ruth 1–4). This does not in any way mean that you should you lie for your husband. The consequence of lying is great before God, so be careful with this, please.

7. A husband needs quality time to be alone with himself and with God. Never forget that God created human beings so that he may have fellowship with them first. You can see the examples of Adam, Isaac, and Jesus Christ himself. The richer a man's fellowship with God, the sweeter his fellowship with his wife. Appreciate your husband for spending time with the Lord; it is for your benefit. Also a man's desire sometimes to be alone is not a rejection of you as his wife. In fact, times alone help a husband to regain a lost focus and regain a bigger perspective. Discussion with other men sharpens his thinking (Proverbs 27:17). It is noted that men work better under pressure, but they are not meant to carry their own burdens; heavy burdens are to be shared (Galatians 6:5). Wife, never conclude that you are the cause of whatever is burdening your husband. You should appeal to him to share his burdens and pray together over them. Ask God to give you scriptures to encourage him; do not get offended at those who hurt him.

8. A husband needs a wife who is grateful for all he has done and is doing for her and the family. What your husband has done is important to him; men's priorities are often different from women's. Praise is a powerful motivator in all our lives, seeing how all things work together for good for those who love God (Romans 8:28).

9. A husband needs a wife whose character and good works can be praised by others. Examine your relationship to your wife as she complements your spiritual leadership, your children, your government leadership if you are involved in politics, and your relationship with your neighbours and finally your church. As you can see, all men, whatever positions they hold in society, like to display their wives, particularly when their wives are well educated, beautiful, charming, and charismatic. Be the wife that your husband is proud of at any given time and at any given place.

Needs of a Wife

I am very careful in what I write here as I do not want to create any confusion or a struggle for leadership of the marriage. I have maintained from the start of *Getting to Know You* that husband is the head of the wife just as Jesus Christ is the head of the church. There is no complacency to make the blood run cold when I talk about what a wife needs from her husband. The love is nonnegotiable, just as the love of Jesus towards the church. So let us look at what a wife needs from her husband. Given all that a husband expects from his wife, the wife expects the same from her husband.

1. A wife needs from the husband the stability and direction from scripture and the confidence that he has a growing relationship with God. Every wife will enjoy being the wife of a man fulfilling God's purposes and destiny for his life, prospering in the things of God placed in his hands. She wants consistency in all he does as that provides her security and strength—and the man shows love in whatever is done.

2. A wife needs to know she is meeting vital needs in her husband's life and in his work that no other woman can meet. I have mentioned earlier, and I repeat it again here, that the most devastating action of a husband is to give special tasks to some other woman to do, and that includes his mother, his sister, or some other family member. You must first learn to share with your wife before anyone else. You will be winning her love more by sharing your failures or challenges with her and needing her help even if it is just listening to you and telling you, "Dear, all will be well." Basically there are certain things only a wife can do for her husband. She is a mirror of his present spiritual condition, and she provides power potential in prayer if he will allow her. And many times, a man's wife is his "alarm system" against other women with wrong motives.

3. A wife needs to see and hear that her husband cherishes her and delights in her as a person. She is the only person who can give you physical fulfilment and joy without guilt and the judgement of God. And again, she is a safety valve against hasty, impulsive, or dangerous decisions which can harm the whole family. So to cherish your wife means to see greater value in her as a person. You therefore want to protect her and praise her

to others, something that wives love very much. Let her know she is a vital part of your world, not just the mother of your children but also the love of your life. Never be tired of saying that to her, because she wants to hear it if possible twenty-four hours a day. The secret that I have learnt through my wife is that I must help her with her past, dealing with it from God's perspective. If a woman has been abused by a man before, she is probably withdrawn in many things, but a constant reminder of God's Word helps her to deal with these "negatives" from God's perspective. She develops an inner radiance and a message to give your children and others the same confidence (Romans 5:3–5, 8:28–30).

4. A wife needs to know that her husband protects her and understands her and her limitations. Even though many wives do not admit it, they yearn for a husband who will understand their strengths and weaknesses and who will provide loving and firm direction with wisdom and understanding on how to deal with these concerns of hers. A wife is susceptible to any man who listens to her, understands her, and encourages her and will be frustrated with you as her husband if you don't do these things. She wants to know you support her in all areas of life and that you are proud of her efforts to do well, and she wishes for you to praise her for her accomplishments. You can imagine how glad my wife was when I told her I was very proud of her passing her examination to upgrade her diploma for her nursing promotion course. It is not easy studying at an advanced age with children and other family responsibilities, but she did it, and I am very proud of her. I will include it in *Getting to Know You*: Sandra, I am truly proud of you.

   What about those difficult days of the month for your wife, like during her periods with severe pains? Do you show care or concern? I have heard stories of how difficult it is for some women with severe pain, irritation, and anger, yet in those periods, they hunger and thirst for the love of their husbands. Your wife needs you to be compassionate, caring, and helpful during her monthly periods. She does *not* need counsel or correction during that time. This is also true during some months of pregnancy and during the wearying period of taking care of a young baby.

5. A wife needs to have her husband set up and enjoy quality time and intimate conversations with her. One of the most basic needs of a wife is deep conversation. Many husbands are not good at this, but you have to be seen as doing your best to give quality time to your wife. Her enjoyment is in knowing you are listening and are anxious to hear her.

6. A wife needs to know her husband is aware of her even when his mind is on other matters, and that she is the most important person in his life. She needs to feel that her husband will put her before the children, his family, his friends, his career, and even his reputation if need be. This is the security her parents gave her, and she now needs it from you as the man. I am sure this is why Eve was created from Adam's rib. Your wife needs to know that you know she is an integral part of you. Your awareness of that tells her she is important to you.

7. A wife needs to feel that her husband will put her before his career. A career will come and go, but your wife is the only person God says you are to be one with as long as you

both shall live. Your wife many times can help you walk through a difficult challenge related to your career, so put her first.

8. A wife needs to see her husband making investments in her life that will expand her world and fulfil her gifting (Ephesians 5:27–29). As God helps your wife to solve her problems, encourage her in the ways she can share her insights with others, helping her to develop her abilities within the boundaries of her primary responsibilities to you and the family. Otherwise the separation of her life into family and work, or family and school, will cause feelings of failure and insecurity. From a Christian point of view, learn her spiritual gifts and discern her progress. Help her in developing them. My wife loves singing, even though she does not yet have the courage to sing in the church. But she does sing at home to the family, and we enjoy it.

9. A wife needs a husband whose character and whose conduct, in whatever he does, is above board. This way, she may talk proudly and boast about him. The crowning glory of every wife is to have a reliable husband in all senses of the word, the pillar that keeps the family together. You can now understand the tragedy when the breadwinner in the family is taken away early in the marriage; life most of the times is never the same afterwards. It is like starting the journey all over again. The joy of the woman is to have her man until death do them part amid whatever circumstances may be.

10. I asked a great woman of God whose husband had gone to be with the Lord why she hadn't remarried. She laughed and said two things: first, "I cannot share the love I had for him with another man. He was my soulmate. He was everything to me, and when he died, a part of me died with him," and second, "He left me with so much—wealth, children, ministry, and properties—that I won't have a desire for anything again, so all I do now is to keep his memory alive." What a testimony of love in a godly marriage. Not even death could put the love asunder; today she shines in God's glory with her children and grandchildren.

CHAPTER 27

Forgiveness in Marriage

This work would not be complete, and no justice done to all I have written, if I did not touch on the subject of forgiveness in marriage. This is one word that we need to have in our marriage dictionary, often to be used whenever one needs it. It should not be far away from you; it should be the most common word for both husband and wife. What is forgiveness? The word *forgive* means "to wipe the slate clean, to pardon, to cancel a debt". When we wrong someone, we seek his or her forgiveness in order for the relationship to be restored. It is important to remember that forgiveness is not granted just because a person deserves to be forgiven; it is a demand for reconciliation between two persons. Where else to show an example of forgiveness than in a marriage? The Bible speaks so much about forgiveness, including what God says about forgiveness. Examine some of these scriptures: Matthew 5:9, 6:14–15; Romans 6:23; James 3:18; and 1 Peter 5:5–6.

How does one ask for forgiveness? The simple fact is that you must accept full responsibility for having done wrong. "I was wrong. I should not have …" Or "I'm sorry that I …" Don't make excuses. An excuse will often start with the word *but.*

Forgiveness has to do with expression of genuine regret ("I am sorry I hurt you") and genuine sorrow ("I am going to change"). Asking for forgiveness demands the decision of your spouse to accept the fact that he or she is dealing with forgiveness in marriage. I imagine that if forgiveness were more prevalent in marriages today, many marriages would be saved from divorce. I know that for some readers you are already angry about this chapter because you have one thousand reasons not to forgive your spouse. I still want to encourage you to give forgiveness a chance in all circumstances. On the other hand, if your spouse is not willing to forgive you for something, it may be because he or she senses a lack of sincerity on your part. Therefore, evaluate yourself and convince yourself that you are truly sorry for what you have done and what you are asking forgiveness for.

God is the author of forgiveness; it all starts with him and ends with him. Ask God first for forgiveness, and pray that he will also touch the heart of the person you have wronged to have it upon his or her heart to forgive you. Forgiveness is a progression. It does not happen overnight. It may take some time, but you have to make an effort towards doing it.

Forgiveness has several dimensions, so I cannot give you a comprehensive method on how to ask for forgiveness, but using my own experience, I will touch on some areas for which you may require forgiveness from your spouse. Sometimes you need to correct a wrong. Ask, "Is there anything I can do to make up for what I did wrong?"

How does one ask for forgiveness? The simple fact is that you must accept full responsibility for having done wrong.

Acknowledge the pain your action or inaction has caused the other person, or people, in the process. Jesus Christ accepted all our sin and all our pain and all our sorrow, yet he forgave us so that we could have a better life today. According to 1 Peter 4:8, it isn't the little stuff we forgive— love ignores the little things. It is the big stuff that requires forgiveness. In fact, forgiveness has everything to do with love. If you love, you will learn to forgive. Never forget to consider that if you were on the other side, would you expect to be forgiven? So why won't you forgive others? We should realize that Jesus Christ has forgiven us, and that is why we can forgive as well (Isaiah 43:25). One of the obstacles against forgiveness is constant remembrance of what the other person did to you, the reminder of the hurt or pain. The devil is an expert on that. You will need to quit playing the video in your mind of what has been done to you, never to bring it up again. Then God can bring the healing. Forgiveness is like saying, *I give the other person full acceptance, favour, and love.* This does not mean or imply that you approve or that you are allowing the person to continue in his or her sinful ways, but it is the showing of love that surpasses all human understanding. Matthew 18:15–17 and Galatians 6:1 talk about the importance of confronting sin so that your heart is full of love for the other person, not resentment.

Probably the biggest areas of lack of forgiveness in marriage are sexual sin or infidelity; drug abuse; molestation; continuous violation, both physical and mental; and ultimately violation of the Word of God and his principles. If one of these applies to your situation, then you need to follow Matthew 18 and take the matter to the pastor or elders of your church. Don't be silent about it. Instead, deal with it. These things not only destroy the people involved, but also bring reproach to our God. They are also too difficult for one person to deal with or handle alone to bring about changes; you and your partner need help.

If you don't bring forgiveness into your marriage, you face the danger of divorce or even things worse than divorce.

Divorce is a subject I refuse to talk about in *Getting to Know You* because I do not believe in it. And after all we know now, *divorce* should not be in our dictionary and should not be the subject of discussion in our marriage.

CHAPTER 28

The Joy of a Christian Marriage

Some years ago, I wedded, and it was an interesting wedding experience. I was especially struck by the support my wife and I received from our church, Victory Outreach Amsterdam then. Having spoken so much about wedding and getting married, I would not be doing justice to *Getting to Know You* if I didn't let you know about my own marriage.

After meeting my beautiful wife and after her accepting to marry me, I started thinking how to make the wedding creative so that everyone would enjoy the occasion. Sandra and I met a Nigerian friend, Tony, also from the Amsterdam church. He was to sing for us a song in a Nigerian language. That was a surprise for many in the audience, but they followed the tune. My wife's younger brother, Ulrich Monsels, walked my wife down the aisle; his two children were the little bride and the ring bearer, making it a family affair. We had just one accompanying crew—the maid of honour and the groom's best man. As I have maintained, you decide how big you want your wedding to be. We wanted ours to be simple and yet colourful. Pastor Jofrey Leito officiated the wedding. Immediately after we tied the knots and were prayed for, the families and guests were allowed to congratulate us in an orderly manner inside the church. We marched to the next hall within the church for the reception, which lasted two hours. After the reception, we were ushered out of the hall and we left for our home.

As bride and groom, we had brainstormed with the pastor on how to insert new and exciting elements into the service, and we enjoyed those elements. In the middle of the ceremony, we included portions of traditional classic Nigerian music. I read a poem I had composed for Sandra. I still remember the title, "The Woman of My Dreams". I never discussed it with her, but it was a pleasant surprise for her and a good one for the occasion. Even those in the audience came up to me afterwards to compliment me on the poem, saying, "I have never heard such a romantic poem on a wedding day before. It was beautiful." On our return from our honeymoon, Sandra and I watched the videotape of the wedding, and then I saw the impact of the poem on my wife, which brought back good memories. I began to hear the words from the poem in my thoughts again; it is a pledge of commitment. I remember thinking, *There is no way to improve on this because the words are so beautiful and meaningful.* I had put a great deal of thought and care into composing those words as a groom needs to do something special for his bride. Be creative. It is just one special day before the rest of your lives.

Today, of course, many young people not only are saying no to wedding but also are rejecting the concept of marriage itself. More and more young people are coming from broken homes, and as a result, they have a fear of marriage and suspicion of its value. So we see people living together rather than marrying for fear that the cost of that commitment may be too much. They fear it may make them too vulnerable. This means that one of the most stable and, as we once thought, permanent traditions of our culture is being challenged—namely marriage.

One of the things I like most about the wedding ceremony is that it includes an explanation as to why there is such a thing as marriage. We are told in the ceremony that marriage is ordained and instituted by God. That is to say, marriage did not just spring up arbitrarily out of social conventions or human taboos. Marriage was invented not by people but by God, and whatever way you choose to solemnize it, either the traditional way or the Christian way, let God be included from the beginning to the end.

We see this in the earliest chapters of the Old Testament, where we find the creation account. We find that God creates in stages, beginning with the light (Genesis 1:3), and capping the process with the creation of man (v. 27). At every stage, he utters a benediction, a "good word". God repeatedly looks at what he has made and says, "That's good" (vv. 4, 10, 12, 18, 21, 25, 31).

But then God notices something that provokes not a benediction but what we call a malediction, that is, a "bad word".

What was this thing that God saw in his creation that he judged "not good"? We find it in Genesis 2:18, where God declares, "It is not good that the man should be alone." That prompts him to create Eve and bring her to Adam. God instituted marriage, and he did it in the first instance as an answer to human loneliness. For this reason, God inspired Moses to write, "Therefore a man shall leave his father and his mother and hold fast to his wife, and they shall become one flesh" (v. 24).

Many young people not only are saying no to wedding but also are rejecting the concept of marriage itself.

As much as I like and appreciate the words of the wedding ceremony, I believe the form of the ceremony is even more important. This is because the wedding ceremony involves the making of a covenant with a witness (pastor). The whole idea of a covenant is deeply rooted in biblical Christianity. The Bible teaches that our very redemption is based on a covenant. Much could be said here about the character of the biblical covenants, but one vital facet is that none of them is a private matter. Every covenant is undertaken in the presence of witnesses. This is why we invite guests to our weddings, so they will witness our vows and hold us accountable to keeping them. It is one thing for a man to whisper expressions of love into a woman's ear when no one will hear it, but it is quite another thing for him to stand up in a church, in front of parents, friends, ecclesiastical or civil authorities, and God himself, and there make a promise to love and cherish his wife. Wedding vows are sacred promises made in the presence of witnesses who will remember them. I pray that you also remember the words that you spoke on that day and that they serve as a reminder to you that you are in a covenant relationship called marriage.

I believe marriage is the most precious of all human institutions. It's also the most dangerous. Into our marriages we pour our greatest and deepest expectations. We put our emotions on the line, along with our feelings, our trust, our confidentiality, and all that is in us for the other to behold and keep for life. In marriage we can achieve the greatest happiness, but we also can experience the greatest disappointment, the most frustration, and the most pain.

With that much at stake, we need something more solemn than a casual promise to one another on our wedding day.

Even with formal wedding ceremonies, even with the involvement of authority structures, roughly 50 per cent of marriages fail. Sadly, among the men and women who stay together as husband and wife, many would not marry the same spouse again, but they stay together for various reasons. Something has been lost regarding the sacred and holy character of the marriage covenant. In order to strengthen the institution of marriage, we might want to consider strengthening the wedding ceremony with a clear biblical reminder that marriage is instituted by God and forged in his sight.

I wish a happy married life to all those who are married, and I say "Welcome with God's grace" to all those aspiring to get married. It is a good thing to do. I wish you all success.

As you have observed, this is not conventional book; it is a very practical one. I would like to hear from you if *Getting to Know You* has helped you in any way. Your story may help someone else whose marriage needs encouragement. Just send me an email at elvisiruh@gmail.com. If you want your story to remain private, I will ensure it remains private.

I hope to read from you soon.

**I wish a happy married life to all those who are married, and I say
"Welcome with God's grace" to all those aspiring to get married.**

ABOUT THE BOOK

Getting to Know You is a guidebook for those preparing for marriage or those who already married. Its purpose is to teach some simple principles that couples might have taken for granted in building a solid Christian relationship resulting in a good marriage.

You are getting to know someone who you think may be God's choice of a marriage and life partner for you. I have put together a discussion of some conduct and behaviours that will help you.

Getting to Know You is easy to read. It addresses many subjects related to getting to know your partner up to the stage of marriage. Also included are a few details on expectations.

It is exciting. I recommend *Getting to Know You* for all singles, for all husbands and wives, and even for your children and well-wishers.

ABOUT THE AUTHOR

Ndubuisi Elvis Iruh, born on 9 April 1965 at Owa-Alero in Ika North East, Local Government Area, of Delta State, Nigeria. He attended Emmanuel Commercial High School, Ilaro, Ogun State; Ogun State Polytechnic, Abeokuta; and Nigeria Institute of Journalism, Lagos, Nigeria. He furthered his studies in Europe, acquiring other diplomas. He has a degree in theology from Victory Education and Training Institute (VETI). He worked for several media organizations in Nigeria, including *Pinko* children's magazine, Radio Lagos, *City News Weekly*, *Razor* magazine, *Razor* evening newspaper, TNT's evening newspaper, and *Weekend Flash* magazine. He also worked for *West Africa* magazine (London, UK), *New Africa* magazine (London, UK), *Trumpet* newspaper (London, UK), and *Insight* magazine (Holland). He became publisher and editor-in-chief of *The Voice* news magazine in August 1999.

Pastor Elvis Iruh is a licenced minister with Victory Outreach International, serving as an associate pastor at Victory Outreach Almere, the Netherlands.

He was recognized with an ambassadorial role for his work with children suffering from autism under the auspices of the United Nations organization. He is married to Sandra Iruh-Monsels, and they are blessed with children.

Printed in the United States
By Bookmasters